D1607994

Kroll on Futures Trading Strategy

Other books by Stanley Kroll

The Commodity Futures Market Guide (with Irwin Shishko)

The Professional Commodity Trader

Cruising the Inland Waterways of Europe

Kroll on
Futures Trading Strategy

Stanley Kroll

DOW JONES-IRWIN
Homewood, Illinois 60430

*From a Declaration of Principles jointly adopted by a Committee
of the American Bar Association and a Committee of Publishers.*
This book was set in Century Schoolbook by The Saybrook Press, Inc.
The editors were Richard A. Luecke, Ethel Shiell, and
Merrily D. Mazza.
The production manager was Irene H. Sotiroff.
The designer was Sam Concialdi.
The drawings were done by Tom Mallon.
The Maple-Vail Book Manufacturing Group was the printer and binder.

ISBN   1-55623-033-8

Library of Congress Catalog Card No. 87−71359

Printed in the United States of America

4   5   6   7   8   9   0   MP   5   4   3   2   1   0   9   8

To Jean and Harry Kroll
With love and respect

". . . in human affairs the sources of success are ever to be found in the fountains of quick resolve and swift stroke; and it seems to be a law inflexible and inexorable that he who will not risk cannot win."

John Paul Jones, 1779

FOREWORD

In John Train's excellent book, *The Money Masters,* he writes about the careers and professional methods of nine great investors. Among them are several stars whose names are well known to all of us—Warren Buffet, Benjamin Graham, T. Rowe Price, Larry Tisch, and John Templeton. There, among this "Murderers' Row" of investors, you will also find the name of Stanley Kroll. Train describes the commodities business, where Stanley made his money, as an "impossible casino." If this is so, Kroll has had some good runs at the gaming table, and they clearly are no accident or mere luck.

In the 1970s, Stanley had a three-year run during which he built $18,000 of his own money into $1 million. And he performed with equally spectacular skill for his partners. It's best to leave the other tales of Stanley's exploits to readers of Train's book. Suffice it to say that they are impressive displays of guts and brains.

I am not a "commodities man" myself. I try to stick to the paths that I understand better, primarily equities and debt instruments. For me, reading *Kroll on Futures Trading Strategy* was an education. The thing that most impresses me about the book is that virtually all the major tenets of Kroll's advice are rooted in a constant regard for discipline and common sense. In short, the best parts of his advice share the underpinnings of any good investment strategy—watch the markets carefully, do copious research, and keep a level head. As Stanley points out, hapless traders act "on the basis of emotion instead of discipline, sentiment instead of logic, and subjectivity instead of objectivity."

Stanley's trading philosophy draws most of its important

principles from a central core that is key to almost all investing—identify the major ongoing trend of each market and trade in the direction of the dominant trend. Most really savvy investors know that this is as much a key of making money in equities as it is in commodities. One of the reasons that Stanley is highly regarded and has done so well is that his feet are grounded in concrete and not in clay.

When you meet Stanley, as I have many times, you are immediately impressed by how *little* this expert on commodities claims to know. This is one of the greatest strengths of most real experts. They don't get overly confident or pretend omniscience. Better to constantly assume that you don't know enough and constantly investigate your assumptions and numbers; hence, another important Kroll tenet—play in the real world. As he puts it, "the need for a disciplined and objective approach to futures trading is a recurring theme in this book." Realistically, it is *the* theme of the book.

Reading *Kroll on Futures Trading Strategy* can do a little something for all investors. It will not make you into an avid commodities trader overnight, but there is solid advice for each of us. For the novice, it brings a sense, stated in plain English, of how these markets operate and what investing "systems" can work well. For the expert, the book contains plenty of details for resharpening already good steel. For the investor in general, Stanley offers a sense of what makes good investors really good—consistent hard effort on research and the discipline to put it to work participating in significant market trends. Everyone with money in any market can benefit from a healthy dose of Stanley's advice.

Douglas A. McIntyre
President & Publisher
FINANCIAL WORLD
New York City
May 27, 1987

The fund manager from Seattle, visibly agitated, had been giving me a hard time. It was a bleak mid-November afternoon in 1985, and he had come to Port Washington to talk to me about his futures trading. As we sat in the paneled salon of my boat-cum-office-cum-residence, he painfully described how he had been whipsawed in soybeans over the past year in a succession of losing trades—despite what appeared to have been a reasonably (down) trending market. Trouble was, he had allowed himself to be influenced by news, TV reports, and trade gossip. Although he had gotten onto the right (short) side of the market at times, he invariably panicked (he called it "defensive posturing") and closed out his good positions at nearly every countertrend rally that came along. He somehow "managed" to hang onto his losing trades during this period, which considerably worsened his already dismal performance. His state of mind during our meeting matched his gloomy track record.

Having gotten his grim confession off his chest, he asked, rather testily, what my trading system had done in beans over the period. "It's been short since June 11," was my response. "June 11? What's so great about that," he managed to grumble, mentally calculating the time interval as being just five months. "June 11 of *1984*," I replied. A long silence ensued. We both knew that, having been continuously short of soybeans for the past 17 months, the profit in the position exceeded $10,000 per contract.

Regrettably, this sort of conversation has been repeated countless times over the past 30 years, leading me to the inescapable conclusion that each trader's worst enemy is neither the market nor the other players. It is he, himself . . . aided and abetted by his misguided hopes and fears, his lack of discipline to trade with the trend and to allow profits to run while limiting losses on bad positions, his boredom and inertia, his apparent need for "action," and his lack of confidence in his own (frequently correct) analysis and trading decisions.

Someone once said that the surest way to make a small fortune in futures trading is to start with a large fortune. Unfortunately, there is considerable truth in that bit of cynical logic. Clearly, the losers outnumber the winners by a substantial margin. So what is it that continues to attract an increasing number of investors to this game? For me, it is the knowledge—confirmed by nearly 30 years of personal experience—that the futures market is clearly the best way for an investor *to have the opportunity* to parlay a modest initial stake into a substantial fortune. For a trade firm or financial institution the futures markets present a means of laying off (hedging) financial risks and, in fact, *having the potential* to make a profit on dealings that would otherwise be a sure loss. Countless family fortunes and international mercantile empires had their humble beginnings in canny and profitable commodity dealings.

But surely it takes far more than desire and wishful thinking for the operator to break into the winners circle. To be successful, an investor must be practical and objective, pragmatic and disciplined, and, above all, independent and confident in his analysis and market strategy. One maxim, which has consistently guided me during scores of trading campaigns, comes from Jesse Livermore, perhaps the most successful lone market operator during the first half of this century: "There is only one side of the market, and it is not the bull side or the bear side, but the right side."

I've spent my entire professional career as a practitioner in quest of speculative profits. But I still consider myself both student and practitioner for, in reality, you never stop learning about markets, price trends, and trading strategy. After all these years, I'm still concerned with the quest for profits—no, for *substantial* profits—from the markets. Considering the tremendous financial risks involved, the emotional strain, and the feelings of loneliness, isolation, self-doubt, and, at times, sheer terror which are the futures operator's almost constant companions, you shouldn't be content with merely making "profits." Substantial profits must be your goal.

That is what this book is all about. It's about the strategy and the tactics of seeking substantial profits from the markets. It's about getting aboard a significant trend near its inception and riding it to as near to its conclusion as humanly possible. It is about making more on your winning trades and losing less on your losers. It is about pyramiding your winning positions to maximize profits while keeping losses under control.

It is my belief, confirmed in the real world of tens of thousands of trades made by hundreds of traders, that viable money management strategy and tactics are as important to an overall profitable operation as a first-class trading system or technique.

And, although I would ideally prefer to have both, my priority would be for the best in strategy and tactics. You will do better, in my opinion, with first-class strategy and tactics and a mediocre trading system than the reverse. A significant portion of this book will be concerned with elaborating on that premise because I consider first-class strategy and tactics as the linchpin of any successful trading campaign.

One final word before you embark on this work. Readers may write to me, in care of the publisher, about any aspects of this book they would like to discuss further. I will respond to the best of my ability and time availability.

Stanley Kroll

ACKNOWLEDGMENTS ————————————————

I would like to express my sincere appreciation:

To Commodity Research Bureau, Inc., and Gerald Becker, publisher, for permission to reprint charts and tables from their very fine publications. To Seymour Gaylin, production editor, and to Wanda Hardy, senior administrative assistant, for supplying me with countless back copies of charts.

To Jake Bernstein, publisher of MBH Commodity Advisors, Inc., for permission to reprint his excellent seasonal charts.

To Darrell Jobman, editor-in-chief of *Futures* magazine, for permission to reprint, in Chapter 18, portions of an article I wrote for the magazine.

To Edward Dobson, president of Traders Press, Inc., for permission to reprint portions of their edition of *Reminiscences of a Stock Operator*, by Edwin Lefevre.

And especially to my editor, Dick Luecke, who, in the process of editing my copy, provided me with a first-class "course" in the craft of book writing.

Much of the content of this book has been drawn from the biweekly column on commodities that I have written for Financial World *magazine for nearly five years. I would like to gratefully acknowledge* Financial World's *cooperation in allowing much of that material to be used here.*

CONTENTS _____

LIST OF CHARTS AND TABLES

*CRB stands for Commodity Research Bureau.

---

†MBH stands for MBH Commodity Advisors, Inc.

PART ONE

Strategy and Tactics in Futures Trading

CHAPTER ONE

What Is Trading Strategy and Why Is It Important?

During my boyhood in the 1940s, one of the great attractions of each Saturday afternoon was going to the movies, younger brother in tow, with 75 cents in my pocket to cover admissions and goodies. In that simple bygone world, the Saturday afternoon serial provided a full measure of fantasy and excitement and kept us coming back each week for more of the same.

Well, it's 40 years later, and the Saturday afternoon serials are gone. I now have for my weekly excitement the ongoing "serial" of commodity speculation. It is the key to fantasy and riches. It is forever "to be continued," and players breath a sigh of relief each evening and wonder what triumph or disaster will befall them tomorrow. We traders are the players in this ongoing drama. What we have lost in innocence, we have gained in experience, in intensity, and in a continually renewed determination to come out as one of the fortunate few to make a killing in the market. We strive to emerge with skin and purse intact, if not enhanced, and to ride off into the sunset of fast cars, old houses, or large boats, and with a personal universe of people who sincerely care about one another.

But first things first—we still have to beat the market, don't we? For starters, we must focus on the fact that we are speculators, not gamblers. We study each market situation, both historical and current price action, concentrating on either the technical or fundamental market factors, or a balance of the two. We then

3

must formulate a strategy that encompasses contingencies for both profitable *and* adverse positions—and all this must be done *before* entering the market. Furthermore—and this should be paramount—we do not trade for the *action*, the excitement, or to entertain friends with wild and woolly anecdotes. We accept the high risks for just one reason: to make a big score.

Back in 1967, I received the following letter, quoted in part below:

> A New York friend sent me your World Sugar Market Letter of October 17, which I found interesting and subsequently quite profitable. . . . The quotation from Jesse Livermore reminded me of my late lamented father, when I asked him as a boy how you made money on the futures market. His answer, "You have to be bold and you have to be right." I then said, "What if you are bold and wrong?" and he said, "You just go down with the ship."
>
> He did just that, unfortunately.

My continuing dialogue with commodity speculators and hedgers via telephone, correspondence, in person, and even international Telex has been an enjoyable and rewarding aspect of my career and one I have always taken seriously. In reflecting on these myriad contacts, one recurring theme seems to surface. Even the *least* successful traders occasionally experience the big profits that are there in the market—elusive and tough to capture, but there. And, if you can avoid the considerable hazard of the big wipeout, you will take home the big profits. But how do you avoid the disaster, the big wipeout, that is all too common in the world of the commodity trader? Or, as expressed more poignantly in the letter above, how do you avoid going down with the ship?

Ever since people got together and bartered stone tablets, spears and hatchets, or something to eat, there have been winners and losers in the commodity game. Yet, despite the obvious profit potential and the high leverage,[1] most speculators—including many professionals—end up losers. Many lose in a big way.

Aside from the small number of professional floor operators, who scalp in big volume from the exchange floors and pay negligi-

---

[1]Commodity positions can be put on with as little as 6 percent or less of the contract value.

ble clearing fees, the traders who make big money on any sort of consistent basis are the longer-term position traders. They tend to be trend followers.

I have been fortunate to have been on the right side of some big positions and big profits, some of them held for as much as 8 or 10 months. In summarizing the tactics you need to avoid the big wipeout and to stand proudly in the winner's circle, the following constitutes the essence of a basic strategy:

1. Participate only in markets that exhibit strong trend-adhering characteristics or that your analysis indicates are developing into a trending formation. Identify the major ongoing trend of each market and trade in the direction of this dominant trend or stand aside (see Figure 1–1).

FIGURE 1–1   December 1986 Corn: A Clear-Cut, Major Bear Trend
The primary element of trading strategy is to identify the major trend of each market and to trade in the direction of that trend. Your with-the-trend position could result in a big move, so try to stay aboard for the ride. Assuming you can control losses on adverse positions, you only need a few good moves like this a year to reap big profits.

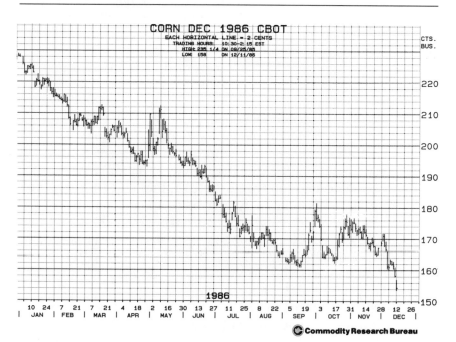

CORN DEC 1986 CBOT
EACH HORIZONTAL LINE = 2 CENTS
TRADING HOURS: 10:30-2:15 EST
HIGH 235 1/4 ON 09/25/85
LOW 158   ON 12/11/86

CTS.
BUS.

1986

| 10 | 24 | 7 | 21 | 7 | 21 | 4 | 18 | 2 | 16 | 30 | 13 | 27 | 11 | 25 | 8 | 22 | 5 | 19 | 3 | 17 | 31 | 14 | 28 | 12 | 26 |
| JAN | | FEB | | MAR | | APR | | MAY | | JUN | | JUL | | AUG | | SEP | | OCT | | NOV | | DEC | |

Ⓒ **Commodity Research Bureau**

2. Assuming that you are trading *in the direction of the trend*, initiate your position on either a significant breakout from the previous or sideways trend or on a reaction to the ongoing major trend. That is, in a major downtrend, sell on minor rallies into overhead resistance or on a 45 to 55 percent rally (or third to fifth day of the rally) from the recent reaction bottom. In a major uptrend, buy on technical reactions into support or on a 45 to 55 percent reaction (or the third to fifth day of the reaction) from the recent rally high. In this regard, it is imperative to note that, if you misread or choose to ignore the trend and are buying against a major downtrend or selling against a major uptrend, you are likely to spill considerable amounts of red ink.

3. Your with-the-trend position could result in a big, favorable move, so remain aboard for the ride. Resist the many temptations to trade minor swings and to scalp against-the-trend positions, unless you are very experienced at doing so *and* you use close and consistent stops.

4. Once the position is going your way and the favorable trend has been confirmed by market action, you can add to the position (pyramid) on technical reactions as noted in 2 (above).

5. Maintain the position until your objective analysis indicates that the trend has reversed or is reversing. Then close it out and fast! Subsequent chapters will discuss the specific and detailed tactics of exiting a position. Briefly, you can do it with trailing stops, on the basis of a computer trend-following system that signals a "flip" in trend, or on the failure to hold following a 45 to 55 percent countertrend reaction. If subsequent market action tells you that the major ongoing trend is still intact and that you have liquidated prematurely, get back aboard; but do it carefully and objectively, again initiating with-the-trend positions on technical reactions against the minor trend.

6. But what if the market moves adversely, not with you (like it's supposed to do)? First of all, how do you know that it's a bad position? The margin clerk or your daily equity run will tell you this in no uncertain terms, even if you refuse to admit it to yourself. Dickson Watts, the famous turn-of-

the-century cotton speculator, once said, "Run quickly or not at all." He may have had sufficient money or been enough of a masochist to include the "or not at all" portion of this admonition. My advice is to take his advice, minus the "or not at all."

The necessity of a first-class, viable strategy is self-evident. It is no less relevant here than in chess competition, tournament tennis, marathon running or corporate takeovers. The common denominator lies in the fact that success or victory involves both technical as well as strategic considerations. With players often equally qualified and experienced in the technical aspects of their trade or endeavor, what distinguishes the winner from the loser is the consistent and disciplined application of first-class strategy and viable tactics.

The correct utilization of good strategy is especially important in futures trading. Indeed, we all know the basic rules, don't we? Take the traders who have never had a winning year no matter how long they've been at it (unfortunately, I'm describing the majority of speculators). Yet they've surely heard and can probably recite verbatim some of these good old maxims—"the trend is your friend," "cut your losses short and let your profits run," "the first loss is the cheapest," and so forth. Here is winning strategy in its most basic form. And, while consistent winners share a single-minded adherence to these basic strategies, consistent losers are just as single-minded in their avoidance and violation.

Finally, while a consistent viable strategy is clearly the mainstay of successful operations, three additional traits are required: *discipline*, *discipline*, and *discipline*. The balance of this book is devoted to presenting and proving these thesis. And I can attest from personal (and painful) experience that whenever I was careless or foolish enough to stray from these tenets, I lost money— sometimes lots and lots of money. It should come as no great surprise that I generally made money when operating according to the strategies and tactics set forth here. These are universal experiences.

CHAPTER TWO

A Good Technical System Is Just Half What You Need

A few years ago, I addressed a gathering of some 600 investors at a technical trading seminar in New Orleans. It was a three-day meeting sponsored by the Technical Analysis Group, also known as Compu-Trac—an excellent organization whose annual seminar is designed to help members acquire a better understanding of technical trading tools and to examine the latest studies of market behavior. The topic of my address concerned the steps you need to focus on after you've developed or acquired a good technical trading system: viable market strategy and tactics combined with sound money management.

It is the combination of the two—the technical trading system *and* the sound strategy and tactics—that can put you in the ranks of the consistent winner. And they can keep you there most years.

Many traders feel that they can beat the markets with a good technical system or a good charting approach. In fact, a good technical system, or even an accurate trend projection, is only half of what is required for success. It is not enough to accurately identify a market trend or the price objective of a given move— and that itself is tough to do. You still have to resort to a viable strategy in order to maximize the profits on your winning positions and minimize the losses on your adverse ones.

This was brought home to me a number of years ago when I was operating my own clearing firm at 25 Broad Street in lower Manhattan. I met with some clients who were professional traders to formulate a strategy for garnering real profits from the market over the coming months. They operated as a little trading group and had been consistently losing due to their short-term focus, their lack of discipline in timing of trades, and their total disregard for any kind of consistent or viable market strategy. After reviewing a number of markets and projecting probable trends and price objectives, I suggested cocoa as the market to be in over the coming months. Cocoa was then trading around the 12.00 level, and I offered the thesis that we could see the market advance into the low 20.00s. We were unanimous in that analysis (which, knowing what I now know, should have gotten me very nervous). We commenced our bull operation that afternoon, with each of us picking up an initial long position around the 12.00 mark.

We were right. Over the coming months, Cocoa did get up to the 22.00 level! And I made some money on the deal, although not as much as I should have for being so accurate in my analysis. What of my colleagues? Well, over the six-month period, they actually ended up losing nearly $200,000. How could that have happened? They started buying at the 12.00 level, had correctly projected the price to the low 20.00s, and had sold off their final long contracts right up at that level. So what went wrong?

Well, they started the campaign as cautious buyers (I couldn't figure that out, as they had plunged heavily in nearly all their other losing plays) and kept increasing the size of their buy orders as the market advanced from 12.00 to 15.00. Unfortunately, their position resembled an upside-down pyramid, and at the very first technical reaction, their account went into a big loss. When the margin clerk sent his familiar greetings, they panicked, dumping their entire position. If that weren't dumb enough, they committed the classic blunder! They went short, reasoning that they would take advantage of the downswing to recoup their recent heavy losses. Short on a technical reaction in a major bull market! Not surprisingly, they weren't quick enough to reverse back to long when the market inevitably resumed its advance. They took a beating on the short position as well. This typified their trading during the ensuing months. By the time the dust settled and we all sold out our final longs around the 22.00 level, they had contributed some $200,000 in trading losses to the other, not necessarily smarter but more disciplined and strategically superior, players.

Clearly, their strategy and tactics represented the perfect example of *how not to* trade the markets. They zigged (sold) when the should have zagged (bought); they zagged when they should have done nothing but watch the market and count their profits. You can almost profile good market strategy by describing the exact opposite of what these hapless professional traders did.

This little cocoa misadventure is just one of the more graphic examples of the lengths to which futures traders will go in ignoring the most basic tenets of good market strategy and money management on the way to becoming big losers. Most speculators create these disasters unintentionally, but the result is still the same: big losses.

Some time ago, Mr. A. phoned and complained that the trading system he had been using at my recommendation wasn't working. He had just taken a big hit and was down to some 35 percent of his original capital. On the face of it, this spoke poorly for the technical system. His declaration seemed extraordinary to me, since I too had been following this particular system and knew that it had been performing quite satisfactorily. "How much capital did you start with," I inquired, "and what was the largest position you've had since going on the system?" His reply was a real shocker. He had started with $25,000 and his largest position at any one time had consisted of 15 corn, 10 wheat, 1 sugar, 1 cocoa, 2 lumber, 2 hogs, and 1 Swiss, for a total of 12 contracts. I then asked if he had read and understood the manual that accompanied the system. He said that he had. How then, could he have been sitting with 12 contracts when the manual clearly advised a maximum of 6 contracts for the $25,000 portfolio? I also asked him why he was in cocoa when the manual recommended $50,000 as the minimum size account for carrying cocoa. But the most startling aspect of all this was his lumber position, which was the biggest loss in his account. Lumber isn't even on the system.

So why had he done these self-destructive things? And why had he spent nearly $3,000 for a good long-term computerized trading system, only to completely ignore both the trading signals and the strategies? Like most speculators, bad trading habits are difficult to overcome. Bad trading habits? This hapless gentleman obviously traded on the basis of emotion instead of discipline, sentiment instead of logic, and subjectivity instead of objectivity. He allowed his fear of losing to overcome his hope of winning. When the system agreed with the positions he wanted to take, he took the positions. When the system was at odds with the positions he wanted to take, he *still* took the positions. In short—he used his own system instead of the tested and proven one in his computer. His system was deceptively simple—hold on to the losing positions and close out all the profitable ones as soon as they showed even a few hundred dollars profit. He apparently was out to prove that his trading decisions were superior to those of the computer system. The bottom line results confirmed that they weren't. Well, at least he learned his lesson from all this, right? Wrong! He attributed his losses and his underperformance relative to the system to an unfortunate run of bad luck. Can you imagine that?

Lest you think that this sort of experience is just an isolated one, I received shortly afterwards a visit from a gentleman who had purchased the same computer system and had made the mistake of giving it to a professional broker to operate for him. He had done even worse than the previous fellow, having lost about 90 percent of his starting capital of $10,000, and he had some serious reservations. Again, I asked the same opening question and was told that the $10,000 account had commenced trading with corn, hogs, Swiss, sugar, and mini-silver; in some instances, more than a single contract. A cursory glance at the trading summary confirmed what I fully suspected—not only had the starting position been much too large for the capital, but the account had been grossly overtraded. In the presence of this trader, I reviewed his account vis-à-vis the signals generated by the system he thought he had been using—but which, in reality, he was not. I demonstrated to his satisfaction that had he followed both the signals *and* the strategy mandated by the system, he would have been down by only 20 percent. He would have had sufficient capital left to try to recoup the losses and get into the plus column—a far cry from the hopeless situation he was now in.

There is a good, solid lesson here, and it is this: In both cases, the system didn't fail the traders, the traders failed the system—and themselves as well.

There is no single system or technical trading method, nor will there ever be one, that can be a winner all the time. However, a number of solid systems, when used properly and in conjunction with sound trading strategy and money management (and that certainly includes not overpositioning or overtrading), can provide the operator with an important edge in the quest for consistent profits. They enable the trader to win more on his profitable trades and to lose less on his unprofitable ones—and that's a significant edge we are always seeking.

Another important element of strategy that further contributes to this winning edge relates to the problem, and the ultimate decision, of which markets to get into when taking positions. I was recently faced with an interesting market dilemma and would like to share with you both the problem and my solutions. I opened a new account with an investor in San Francisco and was evaluating which markets to put him into. In terms of the currencies, my system had been long the yen for the past six months with a substantial profit on the position but had just recently gone short the Swiss with just a small profit on the open position. I wanted to have a position in a currency, but which one? I decided on the short Swiss, since the position had only recently been signaled and the reversal stop was just 35 points above the market. This limited the loss to some $475 per contract, whereas the stop on the yen position was much further away, equating to a bigger dollar risk.[1] Here is the practical embodiment of one aspect of my strategy which mandates that you do not allow (well, *try* not to allow) a good profit to turn into a loss. What is a good profit? A profit of 100 percent or more of the position's margin.

Continuing with my problem of deciding on the initial positions for this new account, my computer system was short all three grains—beans, corn and wheat. I opted to take just one of these positions. With the grain markets down quite severely and in a rather oversold position, even a modest rally could be severe. I wanted to limit my exposure on the short side of grains. So which one would it be? I would want to be short either the weakest market or the one with the closest reversal stop. The stop on corn was 16 cents—quite a high risk for this relatively slow-moving

---

[1] In retrospect, this strategy worked out well because the currencies did continue to decline. Within a few weeks, the protective buy-stop stop had followed the market down to a no-loss and ultimately a locked-in profit on the short position.

market. The stop on beans was even further at 44 cents. This short position had been signaled some 14 months earlier and had a large profit. Nevertheless, 44 cents, equal to $2,200 risk, was excessive for a new position. However, the buy stop on wheat was just 9 cents above the current market, equating to a risk of some $500 per contract, including commissions. My decision seemed obvious: Sell the wheat. The risk was the smallest of the grains, and, if the market continued to decline as the major trend seemed to indicate, the reversal stop would continue to follow the market down to a no-loss and, soon enough, a locked-in profit. Here is a straightforward example of viable market management in a routine day-to-day situation.

K I S S (Keep It Simple Stupid)

There's this guy I know named Joe, and his motto is KISS. It's not an expression of his amorous nature. It translates into, "keep it simple, stupid," which aptly describes Joe's extremely successful approach to futures trading.

In early October 1985, Joe had been taking good profits on the long side of sugar and the short side of beans. Most of the markets had old and established trends then and were pretty crowded with commission house speculative long positions with a substantial quantity of sell-stop orders below the market. Under these conditions, Joe felt that the markets were pretty vulnerable to a bear raid by professional operators. Accordingly, he didn't fancy sharing the same side of the markets with a predominance of what he considered weak long holders. He was looking for a new and less crowded market to play in, and his attention was increasingly drawn to coffee. Joe characteristically avoided trading coffee— matter of fact, he didn't even drink the stuff! Between the sharp practices of the producing nations, powerful trade houses, and professional floor traders, Joe felt that the outside coffee speculator was playing in a game with a loaded deck.

But events that were shaping up convinced Joe to take a second look at this volatile market. Recent price action revealed that the major trend was sideways, with the market finding strong support on setbacks to the 134.00 level (basis December) and resistance on rallies into the 140.00 to 141.00 zone. This broad sideways trading range had been ongoing since mid-July; in fact, Joe had made a few countertrend trades, buying on reactions toward the bottom of the trading range and selling on rallies toward the top. During the last few months, Joe had reaped some small but meaningful profits. The more Joe studied the technical aspects of this coffee market, the more he came to focus on the significance of an eventual breakout from this 134.00 to 141.00 sideways trading range (see Figure 3−1).

But in which direction would it pop? Joe didn't know. But he did project that, once it closed outside of this range, there would likely be a big move, and he intended to be in on it.

During the week of October 7, the market became very quiet. Like the calm before the storm, this suggested that something big was about to happen. Joe left open orders with his broker to buy a quantity of Decembers at 141.60 stop and to sell at 133.40 stop; in the event of either order being filled, he would cancel the other

FIGURE 3−1   December 1985 Coffee

Between July and October 1985, futures were locked within a tight range from 134.00 to 141.00. Astute technical traders premised that a breakout (on close) in either direction would set the stage for the next big move, and they were right. On October 10, the December future closed at 141.65—the bull market had begun! The market ultimately reached the 270.00 level, basis nearest future, before the move ran its course.

COFFEE DEC. 1985 - N.Y.
EACH HORIZONTAL LINE = 200 POINTS

TRADING BEGAN: 7- 2-84
HIGH: 176.25 on 12- 5-85
LOW: 129.25 on 10- 1-84

The bull market commences

1985

Commodity Research Bureau

one. This meant that he would remain on the sidelines while prices were locked within this broad trading range but he would get aboard as soon as the market popped out of the range in either direction.

Joe didn't have long to wait. On the morning of October 10, the December coffee future opened at 138.80, traded within a 300-point range during the session, and closed at 141.65—up 229 points from the previous close. That was what Joe had been waiting for, and he bought a substantial long line for both his clients and himself between 141.60 and 141.80.

Joe was pretty comfortable with this position because the market had broken out of a broad base area trading range and now looked much higher. The next area of resistance was at the level of the 1984 highs around 160.00 (basis weekly close, nearest future). He would be buying more on stop just above this 160.00 level. But most of his clients were nervous about the position, and, during the following days, they let him know it. Just about all the Street's market letters and advisory services were bearish, including some prominent and presumably well-connected fundamental reviews. And here was Joe, plunging on the long side.

His clients' inquiries ranged from very curious to mild panic, but his stock reply was, "It's a bull market." In mid-November one of his larger accounts, who had apparently read one of these bearish reports recommending shorts, demanded to know why Joe had plunged on the long side of coffee. Joe realized that any simplistic technical analysis would fall on deaf ears and that the caller wanted to hear something that he would understand and could logically relate to the current market situation. Gazing out his window during much of this conversation, Joe could see the bleak, cold skies of an impending cold front—and the logical explanation was then revealed to him! Joe matter-of-factly informed his client that, since we were approaching winter, the first serious frost would damage the trees and reduce the crop. Joe wanted to be long because the frost would put the market up. The pieces did logically fit and seemed to satisfy his client, so Joe decided to use the same story on anyone else who called.

The market did follow Joe's bullish scenario and began a good advance up and out of its broad sideways trading range. On the following weekend when Joe was idling about, he suddenly recalled that Brazil, being south of the equator and in the southern hemisphere, *would be enjoying balmy summer weather in December.* Winter . . . frost . . . crop damage . . . indeed!

Having bought his original line of Decembers between 141.60 and 141.80—and having pyramided twice on the advance—Joe had the distinct pleasure of watching the market soar to over 180.00. Profits were over $14,000 per contract when they expired in December. And the market didn't stop advancing till it reached the 270.00 level, basis nearest future, before falling. That's the end of Joe's "simple" story.

But it's not the end of mine. The very graphic lesson here is that we are traders dealing in a difficult and leveraged speculative environment, and success will come only to those who keep it simple in a disciplined, pragmatic, and objective manner. Like Joe, *I would rather be right for the wrong reasons than wrong for the right ones.*

It is particularly important for traders to keep things simple because just about everything you read or hear about the markets appears to be so complicated. The crosscurrents, contradictions, and contrasts that seem to confront commodity traders these days are more confusing and ambivalent than at any time in my memory. So what's a trader to do?

In December 1985—just when we had accepted the fact that inflation was on the wane—the leading business daily told us that worldwide inflation had actually intensified rather than eased. And then, just as the leading commodity chart service had convinced us that commodity prices were positioned for a gradual across-the-board increase, we read the following in *Newsday* (December 4, 1985):

> A growing oversupply is likely to depress commodity markets until the end of the decade . . . a U.N. report said. Though prices may rebound, the overall recovery in demand will remain weak in major industrialized countries at least through next year.

"At least through next year"—what happend to "until the end of the decade" in the very same paragraph? What's a trader to do?

Every time soybeans have a strong rally, we are informed that the drought in Brazil is worsening, causing unspecified damage to its soybean crop. Predictably, whenever the bean market declines, we are informed that rain or good growing weather is expected in Brazil or our Midwest. Ditto for coffee, which has thrilled agile traders with both a major bull and bear market in rapid succession, both far surpassing anyone's most optimistic forecasts. And what about sugar, another high-flying roller-coaster market. The commentators inform us that rallies are caused by *increased demand* for sugar plus the likelihood of *smaller crops*; and that reactions are caused by *reduced demand* for sugar and the likelihood of *larger crops*. What's a trader to do?

I can tell you what *this* trader does under such ambivalent circumstances. He goes back to the drawing board, which, in this case, means the charts, both daily and long term historical studies of seasonal price tendencies, and his trusty old Kroll/Wilder Long Term Computer Trading System. Combined with these technical tools is a strong conviction, born out of nearly 30 years of practical experience, that a rigorous, objective trend-following analysis, coupled with the discipline to believe in and adhere to the projections derived from that analysis, is clearly the best way to play the markets. The overriding objective of this strategy is to make more on your winning trades and lose less on your losing ones. Pragmatic analysis and trend projection of markets plus a viable strategy are absolutely essential. This was well articulated by Jesse Livermore when he said, "There is only one side of the market, and it is not the bull side or the bear side, but the right side."

On the subject of "the right side," I recently traveled to Los Angeles to conduct a weekend seminar on futures trading strategy in conjunction with long-term trading systems. My presentation was divided into two segments—first, a discussion concerning long-term trading systems whose objectives are capital appreciation within the bounds of acceptable risk and capital drawdown; second, the trading strategies that should be utilized *in conjunction with* trading systems to achieve these objectives.

To say that the two dozen investors at my seminar were sharp and well-prepared would be an understatement. I was kept on my toes for the entire two days and was constantly impressed with the dedication and sophistication that these nonprofessional speculators clearly demonstrated. By and large, they knew their computers and the various logistics of opening and managing their trading accounts. They were receptive and eager to learn all they could about trading systems and concomitant strategies.

After teaching them the technical aspects of how to use the

computer in conjunction with trading systems, I dealt with the other half of the equation—the strategy of successful operations. Here I stressed the importance of sticking to simple and basic tenets of sound money management. Personal discipline, self-sufficiency, and pragmatism are the crucial characteristics of the successful speculator, but they are the most difficult virtues to teach. And, after you learn them, they are still the most difficult virtues to practice.

Part of the equation of successful speculation requires the operator to undertrade, both in terms of the size of his position *and* the frequency of turnovers. Excessive trading involves additional costs of commissions and breakage. Even more onerous, it places the operator in a mental and emotional position totally at odds with the imperative of sitting with winning positions for the full duration of the favorable move. I hold that it is irrelevant to think about the length of staying aboard a position solely in terms of its time duration. "Do you hold a long-term position two months, three, four?" I have frequently been asked. "Nothing like that," is my typical response. You hold a position for as long as the market continues going your way; you let the margin clerk, the trading system you are using, or an objective chart analysis tell you when the market has turned against you (more on this important topic in later chapters).

Clearly, if you can develop the technique and the strategy of sitting with profitable positions for the major move, and have a system or technical method to get you out of adverse positions before the losses get onerous, you don't have to start with a huge amount of capital in order to have the potential for profitable results. Traders who stress accuracy of trade timing, both entry and exit, can start with as little as $15,000 or $20,000. This modest opening equity leaves very little room for error. Nevertheless, the market has always functioned as the great equalizer of wealth, rewarding the patient, disciplined, and able players while punishing the careless and inept ones, regardless of the size of their starting capital. It is possible to rack up a consistent and impressive score from modest starting capital, to which I can attest from personal experience. The annals of finance are replete with true-to-life stories of powerful and wealthy capital accumulations that began from small but talented operations in the futures markets.

CHAPTER FOUR

Winners and Losers

In his memoirs written in 1829, Bourriene recounts an incident in which Napoleon was asked which troops he considered the best. "Those which are victorious, Madame," replied the emperor.

I was reminded of this incident while perusing some notes on the subject of winners and losers in the commodity arena. *The Wall Street Journal* of January 10, 1983, printed a survey of 20 senior commodity specialists and their best investment bets for the first half of that year. Three points were given to first choice, two points to second choice, and one to third choice. The results were:

Buy copper	18	points
Buy gold	16	points
Buy foreign currencies	15	points
Buy stock indexes	14½	points
Buy cattle	11	points
Buy silver	7½	points

Some interesting observations here bear further reflection. First and most obvious, all recommendations were on the buy side. This proved a mistake since, of the top six selections, only two—stock indexes and copper—advanced during the six-month period. Of the remaining four selections, gold and foreign currencies were down, and cattle and silver just managed a sideways move. And, while all selections were biased to the long side, the few serious bull markets during the period—corn, beans, cocoa, cotton, and sugar—were totally overlooked.

Isn't it noteworthy that copper appears so consistently on the list? It was also second selection in the previous (second-half 1982) survey and was first selection in the first-half 1982 survey. The actual price action of the red metal, as well as the composite decision of the successful players, was apparently not affected by its recurring top selection during this year-and-a-half period. The market barely managed a broad sideways move (down during most of 1982 and up during first-half 1983).

The point of this exercise is to show how difficult it is to predict the course of futures prices—even a mere six months ahead. The dismal record of these experts should encourage serious commodity players to note two things:

1. The experts are frequently wrong, and
2. A technical approach to commodity investment and timing, coupled with sound money management and a focus on trend *following* rather than trend *predicting*, are really the best ways to operate for maximum results.

But a thoughtful student of these markets must ask the question, Why are the experts so often wrong; why do so many traders lose money? The answers may be circuitous and often are difficult to pin down. However, it may be constructive to reflect on what I call "the speculators' laments."

With the exception of my 1975–1980 sabbatical, I have spent most of the past 30-odd years in a quiet, secluded office, either on Wall Street or aboard a large boat, with trading screen, phones, technical studies, and other necessary accoutrements at hand. Invariably, my principal focus toward markets has been to try to make lots of money on my favorable positions and avoid getting wiped out or taking big losses on my adverse ones.

I have invariably played a lone hand—and very much by choice, having learned to do this early on starting with my first years as a Merrill Lynch commodity broker. During one particular period, some of the cocoa crowd initiated me into their daily after-the-close sessions at the venerable Coachman tavern in lower Manhattan. Here, the cocoa fraternity used to huddle on late afternoons, with the commercials and large locals trying, by way of liberal quantities of free drinks and even freer market tips, to sucker the commission house brokers and their clients into untenable and unprofitable positions. The lesson from these sessions emerged loud and clear: Not much good comes from sharing trading ideas and market opinions with others regardless of their presumed experience or expertise. The universal truth on the Street is "Those who know, don't tell; those who tell, don't know."

Over the ensuing years, I've occasionally had the opportunity to lecture or teach a course on futures trading. My presentations generally focused on market strategy, tactics, and money management, rather than on a series of market tips on what to buy or sell. I nearly always came away feeling that I had profited by each such experience, that I had expanded my knowledge or understanding of my chosen profession.

Perhaps the most memorable of these events was a series of trading seminars I conducted in Miami, Chicago, New York, Dallas, and Los Angeles on successive weekends. Attendees ranged in age from 19 to 86, with several parent-offspring and, of course, husband-wife teams among the participants. The level of experience ranged from total neophyte all the way to professional floor and upstairs trader. And, although I spoke more than I listened, I did manage to ask a lot of questions. The replies were particularly enlightening.

I discovered a surprising commonality of experiences among the several hundred participants. And the speculators' laments really weren't all that different for the novices, although many of the experienced and professional operators were understandably reluctant to admit to them. Perhaps the frustration most common to speculators, both amateur and professional, is this: "I watch while the market moves in the direction of my analysis; finally, when I take the position, prices abruptly reverse and career in the opposite direction." Will it console you to know that all traders feel the same frustration at one time or another? It is primarily a consequence of inept tactics and timing, rather than a plot by "them" to get you (and me) out of the market with big losses. But how could "they" possibly know that you (and I) just bought or sold and are now vulnerable for a reversal? I was once so struck by a succession of these whipsaws, that I imagined even if I put on the perfect hedge of buying *and* selling the very same future, "they" could still find a way to smoke me out with a loss on both legs of the position. Illogical perhaps, but it sure feels this way after a discouraging succession of whipsaw losses.

A corollary to this lament is this: "I invariably buy on strength near the top of every rally and sell on weakness near every bottom." In fact, the accumulation of ineptly timed buy or sell orders by undermargined speculators, who tend to buy when everyone else is buying and to sell when everyone else is selling, are what makes tops and bottoms—at least on a short to intermediate-term basis. The result of such careless and poorly timed trading is predictable—big losses and small profits, with an overall tendency to red ink.

Do these quotations sound familiar?

- "I told my broker to buy sugar, but he talked me out of it." (Translation: The speaker may have been thinking about getting into some long-sugar but didn't—and, of course, the market went up).
- "My broker called and told me to buy some sugar. I wasn't keen on the idea, but he talked me into it." (Translation: The speaker bought some sugar, and it went down shortly after the trade).

If these quotations don't sound familiar, either you have just started trading or you have a very short memory! These nearly universal quotations express a nearly universal phenomenon— that is, we invariably find a convenient way to rationalize our errors, mistakes, and miscalculations. May I suggest a sure-fire antidote to this losers mentality?

Analyze your markets and lay out your strategy and tactical moves in privacy. Don't ask anyone's advice—that includes brokerage advisories, market tips, and even well-intentioned floor gossip. And don't offer your advice to anyone else. You don't care if Cargill is buying corn, Gill and Duffus is selling cocoa, or Salomon is buying bonds. You stick to your objective analysis and market projection based on whichever method or technique has proven itself viable to you, and you revise that strategy only on the basis of pragmatic and objective technical evidence. Such evidence could be a signal from your charts, from your computer system, or from your friend the margin clerk, who reminds you that your position has moved adversely and that your account has become undermargined. In short, if you do make money in your trading, stand up and take the accolades. If you lose money, you alone take the rap. Obviously, you will need the confidence and the courage of your convictions to trade into or out of a market. If you don't have that confidence, you probably shouldn't be making the trade (except to close an adverse position to limit your loss exposure).

The list of speculators' laments goes on, but they all seem generally related to carelessness or poor trade timing, ignorance of the basic tenets of sound strategy, and lack of confidence and discipline in adhering to a good technical system or trading approach. Serious introspection, then, suggests this thesis: A sound strategy and viable tactics are just as important to overall success as a good technical or charting technique.

Finally, no treatise on winners and losers can be complete without some discussion of *the desire to win versus the fear of losing*. I have never seen this mentioned in any book, article, or even discussion of trading strategy, but the understanding of this point is absolutely essential for successful operations.

A letter that I received recently from a gentleman in Australia focused on the elusive pursuit of trading profits:

> My paper trading has always been far superior to my real trading, and I have been analyzing why this has been so. I am convinced that the answer lies in the simple truth of which is stronger—the desire to win or the fear of losing. In paper trading, there is only the desire to win. In real trading, there is often only, or principally, the fear of losing.

Isn't this the universal experience? Every one of us has been impressed at how much better our paper portfolios have performed vis-à-vis our real money portfolios. The same might be said about the paper and "model portfolios" touted by newsletter and brokerage firms. One of the reasons underlying this excessive preoccupation with the fear of losing is that the speculator usually overtrades, both in terms of the size of his position as well as the turnover activity in the account. It is important—no, essential—that the trader control these urges to overposition or overtrade. My general rule here is that some $2,000 to $4,000 in equity should underlie each futures position. Also, day-trading and short-swing scalping should be left to the professional or floor operator, who is generally well-capitalized and experienced at this type of trading and who pays negligible transaction fees. Patience and discipline are the necessary attributes here, since profits will accrue to the operator who understands *and utilizes* accurate timing, albeit on a smaller scale, rather than to the large trader whose tactics or trade timing are careless or inaccurate.

I have letters from dozens of speculators, many of them novice traders, who have reported two and three years of consistently profitable results from using long-term computer trading systems. The recurring theme in these communications is the necessity of following the system precisely, in an objective and disciplined manner. These experiences can be a source of inspiration to those traders who find the pursuit of consistent profits within a risk-controlled environment an elusive objective. Chapter Twelve is devoted to this subject.

PART TWO

Analysis and Projection of Price Trends

CHAPTER FIVE

The Tools of the Trade

A popular country and western song relates the pithy advice of a traveling gambler. Like Ecclesiastes, which tells us that "to all things there is a season," the gambler reminds us that there's a time to hold 'em and a time to fold 'em—and sometimes a time to get out of town fast! This down-home wisdom is well known and generally practiced by experienced operators because if they don't practice it, they are soon known as *former* operators.

Over the years, I've been amazed at how naive many public speculators are concerning commodity trading. It is so easy to get into the market. In many instances, you just have to contact a broker, fill out some forms, and send along a check. Within a few days you can be swinging in and out of a big line of positions. Because you can trade on as little as 6 percent of the market value, a starting equity of just $10,000 can control a position of some $170,000. While it's exciting to think about the vast profit potential, you must realize that an adverse move of, say, 3 percent could deplete your capital by as much as 50 percent and a 6 percent reversal could wipe it out completely.

And isn't it remarkable that the same person who may have trained and studied for years preparing for a particular career or profession may think nothing of plunging into the futures market? This is frequently done with little training or practical experience, on the basis of nothing more than a whim, a rumor, or a smattering of floor gossip. As a matter of fact, I have seen people spend more time and energy "researching" for the purchase of a camera or TV than for a purchase of a large grain or metal position. The annals of futures trading are littered with the financial remains of many well-intended, would-be speculators.

To continue the above analogy, the majority of novice traders, after a brief but generally expensive series of lessons on the pitfalls of inept and undisciplined speculation, reluctantly join the category of former speculators—sadder and poorer but regrettably not any wiser.

I have always been a firm believer in thorough and organized preparation for every field of serious endeavor, be it surgery, sailing, speculation, or whatever. And granted, the person with a demanding, full-time career or profession certainly can't devote full-time effort to studying and preparing for futures speculation. Nevertheless, he or she can find ways to help prepare for speculative market operations to improve the chances of success.

One of the most effective ways to prepare for your entry into futures speculation prior to risking real dollars—and I hold this to be a universal way to study or prepare for any new undertaking—is through a careful study of books dealing with the technique and methodology of futures trading. In addition, I've often found articles and features in the various financial magazines, as well as the daily and weekly business periodicals, to be helpful. However, I am referring to articles concerning market strategy or articles that focus on general economic or business conditions. I specifically exclude pieces that attempt to predict future prices or price trends because, even if the forecast were correct—and that is usually not the case—you still have to confront the problem of whether it has already been discounted in the market. As a matter of fact, there is an old Wall Street maxim, "Buy on the rumor and sell on the news." This is just another way of saying that by the time the news is made public, it is invariably too late to take any action on it.

I can recall a situation several years ago when I had taken a big position on the long side of plywood for my clients and myself. Within a few days of my initial purchase, I had a visit from one of my larger discretionary accounts, a securities analyst for a major investment firm. He had just learned that I had put him into the plywood. Greatly agitated, he informed me that he recently attended a stockholders' meeting at Georgia Pacific and had heard from one of the officers that they expected the plywood market to remain on the defensive for the balance of the year. As I was thinking of a diplomatic way of inviting him to stop telling me this irrelevant story, I watched in amazement as he pulled from his case the current issue of *Time*. It too offered a bearish analysis of wood and wood product prices. Being by nature a rather conservative investor (I wondered what was he doing in futures trading and why hadn't he told me how conservative he was when he opened the account), he became a semi-basket case moments later. That occurred when I informed him that his plywood position was even bigger than he thought because I had closed out a nontrending grain position and had pyramided into more plywood.

It took a while to calm and relax him because, while he was an experienced and highly regarded securities analyst and a partner in a prominent investment firm, he had no previous exposure to futures trading. In the ensuing discussion, I made the following points: I didn't care what the Georgia Pacific speaker said because (a) he was either uninformed about price trends in the wood market, or (b) he was informed but didn't care to share his information with the public, or (c) he was correct, in which case the information had probably been already discounted in the market. In response to his query on why I had bought even more plywood, I told him that the strong market action had confirmed the bull market, that it was the best acting position in our portfolio, and that, by this time, it showed good paper profits. Moreover, it is one of my strategies to pyramid onto the best performing positions while closing out the worst performing.

I was still in semi-shock from the events just mentioned, but the next day brought something that took my mind off the plywood market and the strange meeting with my client. As I walked down the dock to my mailbox, I wondered if the package had arrived yet. The publisher assured me that it had been posted, but as of last evening it was still in transit. Today I was in luck, however, for there it was in the marina office. My pace quickened as I walked back to my boat, settled into a comfortable deck chair, and purposefully opened the wrapping. For the next few hours I was totally immersed in studying and taking copious notes.

What, you may wonder, was the object of this intense concentration? What could have so absorbed me for hours on a beautiful Saturday afternoon? Perhaps a favorite magazine or a long-awaited and sought-after book? The truth is, I spent those hours completely immersed in a large volume of contemporary nonfiction dealing with both national and international events and offering, to those who can read its secrets, important clues to the future. The future?

The title of this fascinating volume was, *Ten-Year Weekly Range Charts*, published by Commodity Perspective of Chicago.[1] When combined with a judicious mixture of concentration, experience, and recall, plus an objective, disciplined approach to the markets, it can help unlock part of the key to profitable long-term trading and investing.

In my experience, the most fruitful approach for the nonfloor operator is long-term, trend-following position trading. Here, the trader eschews trying to predict tops and bottoms as a means of closing out (with-the-trend positions) and reversing (to against-the-trend positions). Chart pattern counts, including the 50 percent return rule can be used, but only as a general guide to likely areas of support or resistance, or to locate areas for pyramiding with-the-trend positions. Instead of trying to predict tops and bottoms, the trader seeks to identify major price trends. He wants to get aboard soon after the trend has been confirmed, on a minor trend reaction against the major trend, or on a significant breakthrough of support (for a short position) or resistance (for a long position)—but always in the direction of the ongoing major trend.

Admittedly, this type of long-term, trend-following trading is not the easiest or quickest way to make a living, but for those who are able to do it while managing to avoid getting killed in the between times, the results can be truly impressive—even running into telephone-number-size profits. In the mid-70s, for instance, my clients and I extracted a spectacular seven-figure profit from the wheat market by correctly identifying the long-term trend (up) and sticking with the position (from 3.60 to around 4.90—pyramiding along the way) for the major portion of the bull move (see Figure 5−1).

But like any good craftsman we do need tools, and the particular tool in this discussion is a well-organized set of long-term continuation charts. The best set that I have seen is the aforementioned collection of *Ten-Year Weekly Range Charts*, published semiannually each spring and fall. First introduced in 1984, the set consists of a series of 30 12½" × 17" charts printed on heavy

---

[1]Commodity Perspective, 30 South Wacker Drive, Chicago, IL 60606

FIGURE 5-1 March 1975 Wheat

This was my final play before I closed my office, packed my bags, and took off for a five-year sabbatical. I commenced the bull deal around the 3.60 level and added to the long position twice: on the June breakout around the 3.85 level and again on the July reaction towards 4.40. I liquidated the entire position on the morning of December 9, 1974, on the failure of the rally. Bullish news that morning should have put the market up 3 to 4 cents. Instead, it opened 2 cents lower. When prices failed to advance following bullish news, I felt it was time to leave the party. Good thing too! Seven weeks later, the market was $1.00 lower.

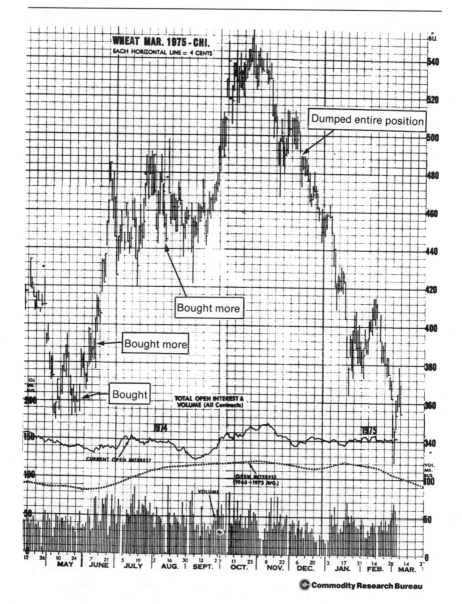

Commodity Research Bureau

stock and spiral bound into a single desk-size volume. Each chart
records 10 years of weekly close price activity. A periodic review
of these long-term charts provides the operator with a distinctly
advantageous viewpoint. The noise and clutter of the marketplace are deleted, and the major trends are clearly displayed for
the astute and pragmatic analyst.

The futures trader also needs a good chart service, and, fortunately, there are several of them available. There exists in some
quarters the mistaken belief that only technically oriented traders need a chart service, while fundamentalists do not. I take
issue with that suggestion and feel that all operators, regardless
of their trading orientation, should include a regular subscription
to one of the chart services as an integral part of their analysis.
These services provide far more than an alphabetized collection of
daily charts. Typically, a service arrives fresh weekly with some
200 charts depicting daily high-low-last prices, volume and open
interest, some form of moving averages, cash or cash-versus-

FIGURE 5−2   Long-Term Weekly (Nearest Future) Heating Oil Chart,
1981−1986

These long-term weekly charts offer a much broader perspective than the
daily charts and can be of great value to the technical trader in identifying and
analyzing major market trends and support/resistance levels.

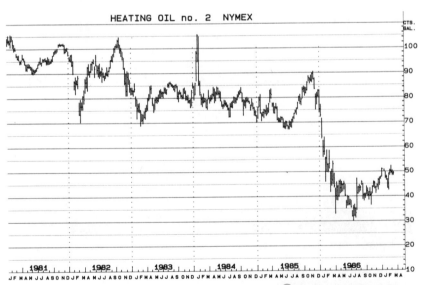

HEATING OIL no. 2   NYMEX

Commodity Research Bureau

futures prices, overseas markets, and a collection of straddle (spread) charts. Included with the chart service, at regular intervals, are long-term weekly and monthly continuation charts going as far back as 20 years (see Figures 5–2 and 5–3). And finally, of particular interest to many technical traders is an oscillator or trend-indicator tabulation, such as the excellent Computer Trend Analyzer and charts furnished in the weekly service by Commodity Research Bureau of New York.[2] This is a powerful aid in

---

FIGURE 5–3   Long-Term Monthly (Nearest Future) Gold Chart Covering 20 Years

Long-term monthly charts, when used in conjunction with weekly charts, can provide the technical trader with the clearest and most advantageous perspective for trend-following position trading.

GOLD COMEX N.Y.   (MONTHLY HIGH, LOW & CLOSE OF NEAREST FUTURES)   DOLLARS PER OUNCE

LONDON SPOT PRICES 1968-1974

COMEX FUTURES PRICES 1975-PRESENT

Commodity Research Bureau

---

[2]Commodity Research Bureau, 100 Church Street, New York, NY 10007

identifying the significant underlying trend of each market, with reversal points noted both above and below the trading ranges.

Especially important for the fundamental analyst or anyone wishing to look beyond the strictest technical interpretation is the *Commodity Year Book*, published annually by Commodity Research Bureau. First published in 1939, this large volume is undoubtedly the most widely used commodity reference source. Besides offering extensive statistical tables and fundamental data on just about all worldwide commodities, the Year Book includes some excellent articles and practical features of interest to all serious traders.

And, last but not least, are the trading systems, predominantly data bank and computer-oriented, which have increasingly come to dominate trading and timing decisions in just about all aspects of futures speculation and hedging. These will be discussed in Chapter Twelve.

CHAPTER SIX

When Fundamental and Technical Analysis Diverge

It was a hot, windless, 1985 summer afternoon in Manhasset Bay. My friend Tony the floor broker and I had been drifting along in his sloop for the past hour, waiting for the two o'clock southerly to come in and send us scurrying over to the North Shore of Long Island Sound for some of City Island's specialty—fresh clams and mussels. Sitting motionless in the still air with the only sound being the slatting of sails and rigging is b-o-r-i-n-g, and, with neither of us being avid conversationalists, we had apparently exhausted our normal subjects. This may have been why we got into the conversation I am about to relate. All my friends know my rule that I don't want to hear anyone's market opinion, nor do I care to give my own. But here we were all of a sudden talking about the heating oil market. Actually, we weren't talking—it was Tony talking and me listening, but why split hairs?

"I'll give you something *very* confidential, but first you have to promise not to disclose it to anyone," Tony whispered in a near-furtive tone. "Look, why all the cloak-and-dagger stuff out here?" I asked. "No one around in any direction for maybe 500 yards. Besides, I'm not interested in your tip, and if you do tell me, I'm going to call everyone I know and say that you gave it to me." Well, that ought to discourage him, I thought.

Wrong! It didn't take him more than a few seconds to recover from that mild rebuke, and he was back for a second shot. "Tell you what," he countered, "I'll let you in on it, but please, don't tell anyone I gave it to you."

He was certainly determined, I thought—it must really be something. And it sure was! "Yamani is shortly going to announce that the Saudis will double oil production." Long pause ensued. "So?" Was the best I could muster under the circumstances. But Tony was clearly not to be put off. "SO? Is that all you can say? Don't you realize the significance of this? When the oil minister of the leading producer announces he is doubling production, the market price will drop $20, maybe $30 overnight. There's a fortune to be made here, and I've just dropped it into your lap. Besides, all the big guys on the floor are going heavily short."

I had heard all I cared to. Besides, who wanted to have this junk ruin what would shortly be turning into a perfectly fine afternoon of sailing. "Look," I snapped back, "I don't know very much about the Saudis and their oil minister or about oil production and its effect on futures prices. And I certainly don't know, nor do I care, about the 'big guys' and what they do or don't do in the market." (I had heard the big guys stories so often I was totally immune to them by now.) "What I do know, though, is that it's a bull deal, and the market looks higher to me. So can we talk about something else, now?" Well, I apparently prevailed, although I never saw this unflappable professional trader look so stunned. But my tactic rescued the day, and the balance of the afternoon turned out just fine.

The conversation was very much on my mind that evening, and I wasted no time in setting out my various charts and technical studies for a careful reexamination of the market. Perhaps there was something in this scenario that I had overlooked or misinterpreted, and a careful double-check seemed a good idea under the circumstances.

It was mid-July 1985, and the heating oil market had been locked within a tight trading range between 70.00 and 73.00 basis the February future. Some of the computer systems had already signaled to cover shorts and go long on July 10, and I just needed a close over 74.00—and the strong market action "said" this was imminent—to turn me full bore onto the long side with the expectation of a major upside move in the offing. Let the big guys and their followers gossip and speculate on the oil minister's announcement and its possible effect on the market. As far as I was concerned, it was a bull market, period! Yamani either would or would not make the announcement—and, even if he did, the bearish news would probably have already been discounted in the market price. And the announcement, if there was to be one, would be the final hope for the trapped bears prior to their being massacred by the strong and rampaging bull. In short, my bullish technical studies told me that we were, once again, seeing the classic bear trap in action.

Discretion being the better part of valor, I opted to sit this bear tip out from the safety and serenity of my long position in February heating oil. And, fortunately for me because, following a few more weeks of sideways backing and filling, during which time the big guys and their hapless followers had ample time to get fully committed on the short side, the market on Friday July 26 closed strong, just below 74.00 for February. That did it! The trap had been sprung on the unfortunate bears, and, following a brief final reaction, the market commenced an impressive rally that ultimately carried some 16.00 cents, equal to $6,700 per contract (see Figure 6–1). What was even more amazing, the Saudi oil minister did, in fact, announce that he would be doubling production (Tony was at least right on *that part* of his story) and predicted a sharp drop in prices. The market, however, was not impressed—in its frantic race towards higher levels, it barely stumbled over the minister's epic announcement. This must have absolutely unglued the intrepid and greatly pained short players, who, in the end, lost considerable millions due to their blind acceptance of a bear tip in a bull market.

There is a very clear-cut moral to this unfortunate story: Play in the real world. Beware of tipsters and other well-intentioned worthies bearing gossip and free advice. And when the fundamental and technical conclusions and market projections are at odds, disregard the technical conclusions or hang onto an anti-trend position without protective stops *at your extreme peril!*

This lesson was reinforced sometime later when, on a trip to Geneva, a Swiss colleague and I were disucussing interest rate trading. "How can your speculators possibly trade these markets on the basis of the gossip and so-called news analyses carried on your TV and newspapers?" he asked incredulously. "Every time some learned expert makes a pronouncement about infla-

FIGURE 6−1   February 1986 Heating Oil
During June and July 1985, the market was locked within a tight trading range between 70.00 and 73.00. Despite major short positions on the part of many floor traders anticipating a bearish announcement from the Saudi oil minister, the market broke out on the upside on July 26, commencing a major bull move to the 90.00 level. This resulted in losses of many millions of dollars to the big guys and their hapless followers, who had been caught in the classic bear trap that they had so often engineered in the past. Their mistake? Following a bear tip in a bull market.

tion or the deficit, about balancing the budget, about higher or lower interest rates, the market almost seems to jump in cartwheels. Why you even have some prominent economist nick-named Dr. Death, whose followers have merely to announce that he will make some speech and the markets suddenly plummet."

Well, I couldn't really disagree with my friend, whose familiarity with our vernacular led him to describe financial futures trading as "a mugs game." Indeed, we have all heard the myriad pronouncements and predictions concerning interest rates and the diverse factors that influence them. For example, talks to reduce budget deficits hit a snag, the Fed is about to loosen (or tighten) credit, the vice-chairman of one of the Reserve Banks says that the economy might be starting to overheat, or an apostle of disinflation is rumored to have altered his projection for the inflation index.

Just about every time that one of the above hits the TV screen or the printed page, the Fed watchers and the financial futures gamblers try to make some logical sense of it and try to equate it with what is happening or what they expect to happen in the market. Meanwhile, the few canny and disciplined operators who follow price trends and objective technical analysis rather than political statements and slogans place their (usually) winning bets, sit back to watch the show, and wonder what the big fuss is all about.

Particularly during volatile market periods, it's necessary to focus on an objective analysis of market trends, both short- and long-term, and to ignore (and admittedly, that's not easy) the hysteria and sounds of alarm that accompany all the learned pronouncements.

I found myself entrapped in this way recently, and I should have known better. There I was, sitting peacefully in front of my charts and my little green screen having successfully resisted, at least to that point, getting suckered into the long side of interest rate futures during a pronounced bear cycle. Going through the daily business paper, I could feel my pulse quicken while reading what the president had said about the ongoing bipartisan deficit reduction talks. Why should I care about all that and, above all, why should that have influenced me to get into the market? Yet moments later I picked up my Chicago phone and calmly bought, at the market, a quantity of T bond futures. Clearly, I was buying against a strongly entrenched downtrend and on a minor technical rally no less. If anything, the order should have said sell and not buy. So why didn't I "lie down till the feeling passed?" In retrospect, I realized that I had succumbed to a combination of undisciplined wishful thinking and wanting to be in that market (it *seemed* too low to sell, I rationalized) at that time. The red ink from that trade will serve as yet another reminder—not that I need any more reminders—that trying to pick off tops or bottoms against strongly entrenched price trends is invariably dangerous to one's financial health.

The need for a disciplined and objective approach to futures trading is a recurring theme in this book. We have all had the experience of relaxing our vigilance, of ignoring the technical picture of the market, which is generally quite clear if we are willing to see clearly. And the results are uniformly predictable, aren't they? I used to think that I knew most of the ways eggs can be served. However, after nearly 30 years in this business, I have come to appreciate one form of egg that, for lack of a better description, can be called "the commodity trader's special." I am referring, of course, to egg on the face, and, at one time or another,

---

FIGURE 6–2A   CRB Grains Futures Index

1984 was a year of confusion and ambivalence for the futures trader. The news and recommendations were almost universally bullish, and speculators bought into the first quarter rally on the assumption that prices were starting to head north. In reality, this brief advance was just a minor pause in the major bear trend that had gripped futures market since 1983 and would continue through 1985-86. Only the disciplined and pragmatic technical traders made money—and lots of it—on the short side of these markets.

Commodity Research Bureau

each one of us has had it served up. It has to be one of the most expensive dishes you'll encounter. And, although the trader tries to wipe it off as quickly as possible, regrettably there are compelling human forces—hope versus fear, greed, impatience, and, above all, lack of discipline—that counter these well-intentioned attempts.

For example, in the autumn of 1984, the Chicago grain markets seemed to be in the process of breaking down from broad sideways trends into plain old downtrends. All of the good long-term trend-following systems had flipped down, as had most objective chart techniques. This was confirmed—as if further confirmation was needed—when the CRB Grains Futures Index broke down through the 230.00 level (see Figure 6–2A). Yet, the reality of this developing bear trend, so strongly entrenched that it lasted nearly two more years, was generally obscured by a steady barrage of bullish stories and articles in the business

FIGURE 6–2B Precious Metals Index

CRB PRECIOUS METALS INDEX (1967=100)

Commodity Research Bureau

press: poor U.S. growing weather and its toll on crops, unprece-
dented Soviet grain shortages leading to huge grain purchases in
the world market, and smaller Canadian crops. Such broad-based
bullish news! So why were the grain markets breaking down into
a tenacious downtrend that would last nearly two years? We
experienced a parallel situation in the metals market commencing around mid-1984, where so many of the eminent market
projections, economic and political analyses, and brokerage recommendations had predicted improving prices and had recommended the long side of markets. Long side indeed! And, here
again, the CRB Precious Metals Index tells the self-same story
(Figure 6–2B). Prices poised on the brink of yet another down-
leg—soon to be confirmed in the market—during the relentless
bear trends of the early 80s.

Digesting such a steady diet of bullish news couldn't fail to
give one a bullish bias—but an objective and pragmatic reading
of the various technical factors showed clearly that we were in a
bearish, or at best a sideways-to-down situation. Successful speculators, with a disciplined and pragmatic approach to their trend
analysis and utilizing a viable trend-following strategy, would
have ignored all that pap and focused instead on a sound technical analysis. By so doing, they would have either scored some
profits on the short side or, at least, been kept away from the long
side and its attendant red ink.

The frequent divergence between what you read in your charts
and system printouts and what you read in the printed word or
hear on TV seems to provide a near-permanent feeling of ambivalence to most speculators. And this applies to projections of general conditions as well. Half of our learned economists keep telling us that, if interest rates *advance*, we will have a general bear
market in commodity prices because higher interest rates increase the cost of carrying inventory and encourage trade firms to
reduce and defer purchase of inventories. Also, with higher interest rates, investors tend to put funds into higher-yielding credit
instruments rather than in risky futures positions. There surely
is logic in that argument. The rub though is that the other half of
our economists tell us that if interest rates *decline*, we will have a
general bear market because it would signify an overall reduction in inflation, meaning falling commodity values; and besides,
investors wouldn't look to buy commodities as an inflation hedge
when they see reduced inflation ahead.

We find the same type of ambivalence when analyzing currency markets, and it is difficult for the trader or hedger to operate in currencies on the basis of fundamental expectations or market events. For example, following weakness in currencies some time ago, the major New York business daily noted, "The U.S. dollar surprised traders with a show of strength yesterday that stemmed, in part, from the detention of a Polish labor leader." The D-mark was weak, and that was attributed to the fact that the German banks are major creditors of Poland.

However, the yen happened to be up that day, so the article deftly labeled its strength a result of the yen's isolation from Europe. However, had the yen declined or the D-mark advanced, you can be sure that appropriately logical explanations would have been created and disseminated.

When I find myself becoming excessively confused or agitated by a plethora of such obvious contradictions and contrived after-the-fact news analyses, my response is to seclude myself for a detailed and pragmatic examination of my short- and long-term charts as well as my other technical indicators—seeking order from among the chaos. Such an interval is always best conducted in some seclusion, away from interruptions and ringing phones, hovering colleagues, and anxious glances. There seems to be a nice correlation between the tranquility of the session and the clarity and quality of the analysis. Where do I go to get away? I sail off and anchor in some snug and tranquil harbor—but a beach, a quiet park or backyard, or just a peaceful and deserted room would do just as well.

CHAPTER SEVEN

Focus on the Long-Term Trends

If it seems more difficult to make good profits in futures than it used to be, the fault is less with the market than with the players. The focus of the technical trader has become increasingly short-term and micro-oriented, due mainly to two factors:

1. Increased volatility and seemingly random price action results from enormous sums of investment money being thrown at markets that do not have sufficient breadth or hedging participation to cope with this huge volume of orders, and

2. The proliferation of powerful microcomputers and software programs that focus on short-term trading swings has convinced many technical operators that this is the new wave of the marketplace and the preferred way to trade.

Indeed, the day of the tick-by-tick computerized bar or point and figure chart, continuously on-line during the whole of each session, is fully upon us. For even a modest monthly outlay, any trader can now have five-minute (or less) bar charts flashing in rapid succession across his screen or printed out. Just imagine trading against a triple "top" created during a 30- or 40-minute segment of a single trading session. That's pretty heady stuff, to be sure. I had a graphic demonstration of this micro-analysis recently, when a trader from Cleveland phoned and asked what I thought about the head-and-shoulders top formation he had identified in the cotton market. I could only reply with, "Huh?" And, after a brief silence, "Uh, what head and shoulders top are you talking about? What cotton market are *you* looking at?" I felt like inquiring if his morning apple juice might have been left standing in the sun too long, but I resisted the impulse. In fact, I had been watching the very same cotton market, solidly entrenched in a strong and dynamic uptrend. I hadn't detected anything remotely resembling a top formation. Under further questioning, the gentleman noted that *his* top formation had occurred during a two-hour period earlier in the session (August 27, 1986). I told him that he was looking at a very minute price consolidation within a strong bull trend and that I wasn't impressed with his analysis. I advised him to look for a spot to buy, rather than to sell. The market apparently shared my opinion, for by the close we saw new highs. This earnest gentleman's triple top formation had been sundered as if it didn't exist—which it didn't! (See Figure 7−1.)

This trader's micro-oriented approach to short-term scalping is the antithesis of long-term position trading, which provides the best opportunity for consistent profits and limited risks. Keeping your primary focus on the longer-term trends allows you to avoid being distracted by daily market "noise" and to maintain a better perspective on price and trend action. How can the trader sitting in front of a five-minute tick-by-tick price chart have any balanced perspective on a market? Three to four hours is long-term to him.

Long-term weekly and monthly continuation charts are essential elements in the position trader's tool kit. I would no sooner trade futures without these charts than I would sail across an ocean without navigation charts.

In addition to giving a clear-cut picture of major trends, these long-term charts provide the ideal view of likely support and resistance levels. I say "likely" because, while there is no sure road to trend and support/resistance identification, these long-term charts are the most effective tool you can find for doing the job. My major copper campaign comes to mind here. It was mid-1972, and my ongoing study of the big picture in various markets revealed that copper had been trading within a broad sideways zone of 45.00 to 55.00, coinciding with a solid long-range support area. The market found good support on reactions into the mid-40s and heavy selling pressure on rallies to the mid-50s. Further-

---

FIGURE 7−1 July 1987 Cotton

Can you imagine—someone seeing a head and shoulders top formation on August 27 on the basis of a tick-by-tick micro-analysis. The trader even went short on the basis of his analysis. His top formation lasted about an hour. This was, in fact, an excellent buying opportunity, especially on the close, when new highs were registered. From that point, it was "off to the races."

COTTON JUL 1987 NYCE

EACH HORIZONTAL LINE = 1.00 CENTS
TRADING HOURS: 10:30-3:00 EST
HIGH 59.45 ON 12/29/86
LOW 32.32 ON 07/18/86

Some head and shoulders top!

@ Commodity Research Bureau

more, a study of copper's long-term price cycle indicated that, since 1964, we had had an important bull move every few years, as follows:

Year	Starting Price	High	Market Advance
1964	30 cents	62 cents	32 cents
1966	38 cents	82 cents	44 cents
1968	42 cents	76 cents	34 cents
1970	44 cents	80 cents	36 cents

I wasn't too impressed with the regularity of the every-two-years thing because that was probably coincidence. Nevertheless, the long-term charts (see Figure 7−2) clearly gave important clues to the big picture in this dynamic market. They revealed that each of the bottoms—the starting point for the big rallies

FIGURE 7–2 Long-Term Monthly (Nearest Future) Copper
During 1971 and 1972, copper traded within a broad range bounded by 45.00 and 55.00, representing a solid long-term support zone. I accumulated a large position between 48.00 to 50.00. The market came out of this trading range heading north on the early January 1973 close above 59.00. It didn't even pause until reaching the 70.00 level. The brief consolidation around 70.00 proved temporary, and by first-quarter 1974, values had reached 1.30 to 1.40. Traders in the mid-1980s, watching the marked mired in the 55.00 to 70.00 range, look longingly at these bull market peaks.

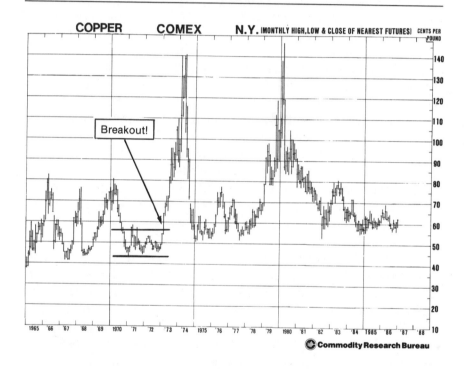

(30.00, 38.00, 42.00, and 44.00)—was progressively higher than the previous bottom. With the major trend still sideways, I went to my short-term (pre-computer era) tools—daily charts, trend-lines, and moving average studies. On the basis of this analysis, I began accumulating a long position in copper in the 48.00 to 50.00 area, ultimately holding some 350 contracts.

One morning, a young man called at my office at 25 Broad Street. He was the scion of an important Far East private banking family, and, after the requisite small talk, he got to the point of his visit.

"We understand that you are a large buyer of Comex copper. May I ask you why?"

"Well, isn't that obvious?" I asked in return. "Because I expect prices to move higher."

He continued his cagey interrogation for a while longer. When he fathomed that I had not been privy to any inside information and was playing this strictly on the basis of my technical studies combined with a long-term strategy, he showed me his bank's voluminous copper study prepared by a team of prominent economists. The gist of the study: Copper was in great oversupply, demand was weak and would remain that way, and prices would continue depressed for at least another year. At that point, I was understandably not feeling very well. I thought that I too might continue depressed for a long time.

Could they be right? My banker friend left me with a copy of his report plus a bad case of the jitters. I left too for the rest of the day to try and calm what was left of my nerves and to prevent myself from calling the floor and liquidating my long position. It took me two days to recover from his little (psychological warfare) visit. Yes, there was too much copper in warehouses—far too much! And it was indisputable that this enormous supply *was* weighing heavily on the market.

And no one could have foreseen—least of all the learned economists who had prepared that detailed analysis—how the copper market could have avoided another year of depressed prices. I couldn't either, for that matter, but I didn't let it bother me. The market action told me, in no uncertain terms, that prices were stabilizing at these levels and that positions were being accumulated by knowledgeable and well-capitalized interests. Ultimately, the course of least resistance would be north. That was my conclusion—my strategy was to hold the long position and to buy more on a weekly close above 56.00, projecting an initial long-term price objective into the mid-70s.

What actually happened was deceptively simple. One day, not long afterward, a Chinese trade group arrived in London, ostensibly to buy feed grains and other agricultural products. But when they left for home, they had bought nearly *all* the copper. And a year later, when my banker friend said he would buy his copper, on the basis of that fancy and credentialized analysis, it was selling at over $1.00.

One final footnote to this campaign. When the ink had dried on our final closeout slips, the total profit on the position came to about $1.3 million.

I receive quite a few letters and calls from traders about various aspects of speculation. But one from a professional trader in Pittsburgh in August 1984 bears special significance as it relates to the subject under discussion:

> We have been hearing quite a bit about the difficulty of trading many current markets. No sooner does the trend "flip" on a great many of the computer systems out there, and the majority of public speculators get aboard the "new trend," than the market seems to reverse again and goes racing the other way. This sort of thing is happening with increasing regularity.
>
> Why is this happening, and what can the trader do to avoid such frequent traps? Unfortunately, many operators use an excessively short-term focus in their technical analysis. As an example, nearly every minor technical rally to an entrenched downtrend, especially rallies lasting a week or more, are suddenly viewed as newly emerging uptrends. In fact, they are nothing more than minor rallies within an overall bear market. Actually, a much better opportunity to sell than to buy!
>
> A case in point is the copper market, where a recent technical rally to the 76.00 level (basis December future) "flipped" many of the short-term trending systems to UP. Weak speculative buying snowballed the technical advance and was actually the cause of the rally. When this buying abated, the market just collapsed and continued its ongoing long-term downtrend. The same for the May/June rally in D-Mark to the 38.00 level (basis September), which suckered so many commission house traders to rush in on the long side. Again, when their buying stopped supporting the market, the downtrend resumed in earnest (see Figures 7–3 and 7–4).
>
> In both of these markets, as in so many others during recent months, brief instances of strength were actually nothing more than technical (corrective) rallies within the context of an on-going major bear trend. Undoubtedly, a longer-term focus, including the use of weekly and monthly continuation charts, and less of a reliance on ultra short-term technical studies, could help a speculator avoid the frustrating and costly style of buying high and selling low that is becoming known as the "oops" approach to trade timing.

This letter aptly expresses the problem of trying to put on

FIGURE 7-3 December 1984 Copper

The early April rally to the 76.00 level was just an intermediate rally in the long-term downtrend. It was largely due to bottom-probing by commission house speculators, with the buying tending to encourage additional speculative buying. The perennially bullish speculators didn't want to miss the beginning of the next copper bull market. The trade was happy to sell into this rally. When the speculative buying abated, the major downtrend resumed, and prices collapsed down to the 55.00 level over the ensuing six months.

long-term trend-following positions, utilizing short- or even micro-term input for trade timing and trend identification. You just have to be consistent. For long-term trend-following investing, use long-term tools—weekly and monthly charts, seasonal studies, and possibly a good technical system with a long-term focus.

There is a related consideration, not often mentioned, that is imperative for successful position trading. It is *patience!* Of all the personal traits necessary, this one stands directly alongside *discipline*, as being essential in any serious trading campaign. In thinking about these personal characteristics, my mind flashes back to a time, many years ago, when a young man barely past 30 borrowed $10,000, bought three exchange memberships (yes, in the late 60s, $10,000 was able to buy three memberships, with

FIGURE 7−4   September 1984   D-Mark

The May-June rally from 36.60 to 38.20 was interpreted by many speculators as a trend reversal from down to up, and was accompanied by heavy commission house buying. In reality, this was just another intermediate-term rally in the longstanding (five-year) bear market. Knowledgeable technical operators played this as an opportunity to add to shorts, especially as the rally towards 38.00 approximated 50 percent of the previous bear trend down-leg. Their discipline was rewarded; the market collapsed, following the abatement of the speculative buying, and prices tumbled to 33.00 by September.

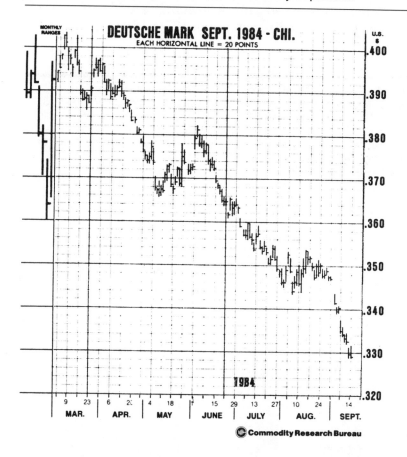

DEUTSCHE MARK SEPT. 1984 - CHI.
EACH HORIZONTAL LINE = 20 POINTS

© Commodity Research Bureau

change left over), and opened his own clearing firm. Eager to establish his reputation as an analyst and broker, he waited patiently for the one "almost sure" market situation into which he could put his clients and friends.

After several months of just executing orders at his clients' direction and writing technical market commentaries, the young man finally found it—the almost-sure situation for which he had so patiently waited.

It was sugar! He checked and rechecked his hypotheses, researched the market the best he could, studied all the charts, both historical and current, and talked to people in the sugar trade. Then, after he was satisfied that this was really *it*, he went to work. That involved writing reports and market letters and distributing them through ads, market seminars, and personal contacts. He worked doggedly, putting in 12- to 14-hour days— and

---

FIGURE 7—5 Long-Term Monthly (Nearest Future) Sugar
Talk about needing patience! I accumulated a big long position in 1967—68 around the 2.00 level, right before it plummeted to 1.33. I lost some one third of the position on this drop, and held on to long sugar for two years before the market broke out of its long sideways range and started moving up. Once on the move, however, the bull market lasted five years, culminating at the 60.00-plus level in late 1974.

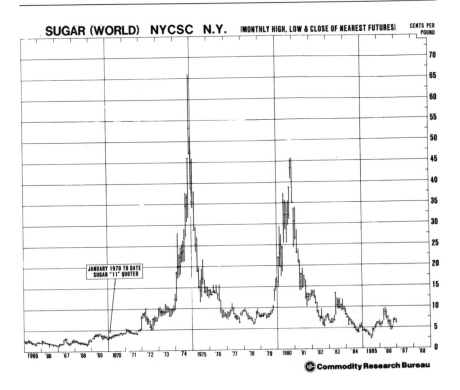

SUGAR (WORLD) NYCSC N.Y. (MONTHLY HIGH, LOW & CLOSE OF NEAREST FUTURES) CENTS PER POUND

JANUARY 1970 TO DATE SUGAR "11" QUOTED

Commodity Research Bureau

the results came in. He had accumulated a large sugar position for himself and his clients with an average price of around 2.00. Just imagine—2.00.

At that piddling price, the young man calculated that the jute bag plus the labor to fill it with sugar actually exceeded the value of the sugar contents. How could he lose?

But he hadn't reckoned with Murphy's Law. Instead of going north, as it was supposed to, the market continued south . . . right down to 1.33! He (I) watched it happen—and the margin calls that week further confirmed the reality of the market collapse—but I still found it hard to believe.

I lost some one third of my position on that little shakeout. But being convinced that the market was at historical lows, having seen the open interest vastly deflate on that professional bear raid, and having examined the long-term and seasonal charts for a further clue to likely long-range action, I had even more confidence in an eventual bull deal. We sat with our position as the market continued sideways. We weren't losing money except for the rollover costs as each future expired. Finally, salvation and big profits arrived in the guise of the massive bull market that started in 1969 and culminated at the 60-plus level in 1974 (see Figure 7–5). What a ride that was! It was also a first-class lesson on the importance of patience, discipline, and a longer-term focus in speculative operations.

The Trend Is Your Friend

It was late July of 1980, and I had recently returned to New York from a five-year, mid-life, temporary retirement. After 16 years in the front-line trenches of trading, I needed the change of scenery and the relaxation as a way of recharging my batteries. Shortly after my return, I started receiving charts and market letters from an account executive at one of the major commission firms. This person and I had never met or corresponded, and I had the impression that mine was just another name on his cold-prospect mailing list. Nevertheless, he approached his task zealously, and my mailbox was kept full of his firm's mailings and advisories. Although I never gave him much encouragement, he kept in touch over the years, occasionally sending a "special situation" report.

Several years elapsed, and he changed firms in the interim, but I still got a report from him once or twice a year. Incredible persistence! In the spring of 1986, I found myself on Wall Street with some time to spare between appointments and noticed that I was in the lobby of this gentleman's office. So I took the elevator up, located my party, and introduced myself. It seemed strange, meeting him after six years of occasional correspondence. Following the requisite small talk, he asked for my account. I told him I wanted to see the pages recording his client's trades (he could cover the names) before making any decision. He was taken aback at this request but nevertheless complied thinking, I suppose, that I probably couldn't decipher the overall results in the cursory glance he allotted me. He was wrong.

In fact, I was able to decipher the results—and they were abysmal. Here was the living embodiment of the speculators' laments that I write about so often. It seems this earnest gentleman did hardly anything right, and it didn't take any kind of a genius to notice that. Small profits and lots of large losses, rather a preponderance of day trades or very short-term holdings, and this from a person who professed to be a long-term position trader. In reality, he was no different from scores of traders I had met over the years. He knew the rules and the buzzwords of successful operations, but something always seemed to happen between the time he put on the position and the time he delivered his winnings to the bank. In fact, I was almost annoyed by the constant repetition of what had to be his favorite saying (I must admit, I had never heard it before). "And remember, Mr. Kroll, *the trend is your friend.*" I recall wondering, since he wanted the trend to be *my* friend, why it wasn't *his* friend as well. But, from my brief examination of his track record, I concluded that any "friendship" between this person and the trend was purely coincidental—or nonexistent.

As I was leaving, I asked if he would mind checking the day's range in sugar. My technical studies told me that the trend had just flipped from down to up, signifying a possible reversal in the long-standing and pervasive bear trend that had taken this market down from 12.00 to under 3.00 over the past two years. "What's the symbol for sugar?" he asked me, as he tried to punch in the code on his desktop quote display. "How should I know the symbol on your machine?" I replied. "Each quote system has its own symbols." "Okay, just give me a second. I'll ask someone for the symbol. Uh sorry, no one seems to remember the symbol for sugar. It's been so long since anyone traded the stuff."

The feeling started at that precise moment, I think, even before I took my leave and walked down the paneled corridor to the elevator. Granted, it was just a gut reaction, but I came away with the unmistakable message that, yes, we had seen the bottom in sugar. I felt as though some bearded and be-robed prophet had appeared to me in a vision, with the simple and inscrutable message, "Buy sugar, my son . . . buy sugar." Perhaps this was the final confirmation of what my charts and computer studies had been saying since the 17th of July. Although I needed neither this unfortunate account executive nor my be-robed vision to help confirm my view of an important bull deal developing in sugar, I felt that they couldn't hurt either. In fact, this person was precisely echoing the collective sentiments of the large body of public speculators who had been battered senseless (and penniless) trying to find the bottom over the past two years. Most of them would now undoubtedly miss the real bottom because they had either stopped looking or were "gun shy," believing that sugar could never do anything but continue d-o-w-n (see Figure 8–1).

FIGURE 8–1 July 1986 Sugar
Although most speculators would like the trend to be their friend, it is a tenuous friendship at best. When sugar finally made its bottom, during mid-July, few speculators caught the turn. They had been so battered over the past two years trying to pick the bottom in the solid bear market. The prevailing sentiment was one of near-permanent bearishness. The small number of clear-thinking technical traders who caught the turn had the field all to themselves.

SUGAR NO. 11 JULY 1986 - N.Y.
EACH HORIZONTAL LINE = 10 POINTS

TRADING BEGAN:	2- 6-85
HIGH:	6.75 on 2-19-85
LOW:	3.79 on 6-20-85

At last! The bottom in sugar is confirmed

1985

⬤ **Commodity Research Bureau**

Unlike the hapless majority of traders, the successful operator
seeks to get aboard an existing trend—*after* the new trend has
been confirmed by his objective technical indicators—and to remain with the position. For how long? How long is long term?
Those are good questions, and, in truth, the answer cannot be
dispensed in terms of numbers of weeks, months, or years. The
only realistic answer is that the trader must stick with the position for as long as it continues going his way, or until the same
technical indicators that signaled him to get aboard the position
signal him to close out. Weeks, months, or even years?

Absolutely! I have watched successful position-oriented speculators patiently sit with positions for as long as two years,
trading every so often to roll over from an expiring month into a
more forward position. As an example, lots of savvy long-term
operators caught the big short in soybeans when it first signaled
on June 11, 1984, and remained continuously short until December 16, 1985—over 17 months. And the profit came to some
$10,550 (after commissions) *per contract.* Was it difficult to catch
the short? Was it difficult to pick the reversal point 17 months
later? Not really, as both the sale and the reversal were signaled
by some of the computer trend-following systems on those exact
dates. Well, you might note, it can't be as simple as that—there
must be a catch. And you're right, there is a catch. The catch is
that the trader must have and utilize a strong degree of *patience*
and *discipline* in sticking with positions for as long as the market
continues to move favorably or until the technical system he is
using signals a flip. In fact, the majority of commission house
traders who did catch the short soybean trade on June 11 covered
shortly thereafter with just a small profit (see Figure 8–2).

To a high degree, boredom and lack of discipline are the main
impediments to successful long-term trading. It is only after an
operator has learned to sit patiently with a profitable, with-the-
trend position that he will have developed the potential to score
significant profits. Unfortunately, and at a very high cost, the
average speculator is most likely to display his patience and
"sitting power" when he is holding an against-the-trend "losing"
position—just the time when good strategy would mandate that
he close the losing position to limit his losses.

I learned this lesson *for the first time* (because we keep re-
learning it, the longer we play the markets) back in 1960 as a
young Merrill Lynch trainee on an orientation trip to Chicago.

FIGURE 8‑2 Long-Term Weekly (Nearest Future) Soybeans
Here is an example of an excellent trending position. Some of the computer
trading programs signaled short sales on June 11, 1984, and remained short
until December 17, 1985, when a new buy signal was generated. The profit on
this short position, held for 17 months, exceeded $10,000 per contract. Only a
minority of those who made the original sales stayed with the short position for
the full move. Most of the original shorts grabbed a quick profit, missing the
major portion of this veritable megamove. You didn't have to be brilliant to have
pulled this off—just patient and disciplined.

SOYBEANS   CBOT

While spending the day on the floor of the Board of Trade, I
wandered away from my group of fellow trainees and somehow
"attached" myself to the ample coattails of Julius Mayer. Mr.
Mayer, it turned out, was the acknowledged dean, at the time, of
the Chicago grain trade with more than 50 years experience both

here and in Europe. I learned much from Mr. Mayer during this and subsequent visits to Chicago. But, most memorably, he taught me that commodity prices, irrespective of either real or perceived fundamentals, will tend to move in the direction of least resistance. This simple concept—and it really is simple, especially when contrasted with the proliferation of complicated and on-line computer programs on which so much technical analysis is based—must be thoroughly understood, both in theory and in application, by anyone who has serious expectations of garnering big money in futures trading.

So Mr. Mayer said that commodity prices will tend to move in the direction of least resistance, and he's observed this phenomenon in over half a century of market involvement. Actually, it may not be a particularly profound observation. The electrician says that electric current will move in the direction of least resistance, and the engineer says that water will move in the direction of least resistance (have you ever seen water run uphill spontaneously?). If you've ever had the dubious experience of finding yourself on one of New York City's subway platforms around the so-called rush hour, you'll discover that human bodies also move in the direction of least resistance. What Mr. Mayer was describing with this brief statement was that commodity prices tend to move in the direction of the dominant force—as in, more buying than selling pressure (it moves north), and more selling than buying pressure (it moves south). This can be stated in terms of any time interval, from very short term to intermediate to long term. Furthermore, once a major trend develops, it tends to pick up momentum, increasingly feeding on its own strength or weakness. In a major bull trend, as the reality of the market strength increasingly dawns on traders, both through their own technical analysis and the margin calls on short positions, their buying to cover shorts and reposition long will tend to overpower the sell orders in the market. Prices will follow the path of least resistance—they will advance. Likewise, during a major bear phase, as the market moves south, it will tend to gain momentum, accelerated by the capitulation of long traders who gradually, albeit reluctantly, dump their losing positions and possibly even take on shorts. And the longer the main body of bulls hang on to their precarious long positions in the face of a major bear market, the harder and farther the market is ultimately going to fall. Their eventual denouement is inevitable, and this is understood and anticipated by professional and trade shorts, who will continue to press the market everytime it appears vulnerable or they sense sell stops at lower levels.

The obvious question, then, is how can the speculator measure the dynamic forces underlying buying and selling pressure at any given time to provide him with a clue to the direction of least resistance? This may be the $64 million question of trend analysis—the Holy Grail for the technical trader. Perhaps the best work in this area to date has been published by Wilder in his *New Concepts in Technical Trading Systems.*[1] His discussion of "directional movement" and "relative strength" are articulately presented in terms of both theory and practice and are complete with charts and actual examples. *New Concepts* serves as the best starting point for any technically oriented trader seeking to study both the theory and the application of the elusive albeit significant concepts involving market dynamics.

Nearly every speculator has, at one time or another, wondered how the big, successful operators are able to take on huge positions (hundreds or more contracts) and end up enormous winners. Meanwhile, the majority of speculators, holding just small positions, invariably seem to buy or sell at precisely the wrong time, paying dearly for the experience. The salient difference, and this bears contemplation, is that experienced, successful operators can usually decipher when a market is in a trending position (okay to take a with-the-trend position) and when it is in a broad sideways mode (stand aside or play a short-term countertrend strategy).

I've found this to be the case with my own trading when, on two different occasions, I held about 350 copper contracts and 2 million bushels wheat. For the most part, I suffered far less than during other campaigns when I held far smaller (albeit countertrend) positions. Haven't we all observed that when your position is in the direction of the the trend and you are sitting on profits, you cannot have too large a position; but when you are struggling with a losing, countertrend position, even the smallest line is

---

[1]J. Welles Wilder, Jr., *New Concepts in Technical Trading Systems* (McLeansville, N.C.: Trend Research Limited, 1978).

excessive. Admittedly, the operator who holds the large with-the-trend position must still contend with recurring technical reactions. But these are to be expected, and he must have sufficient financial and emotional staying power to survive these shakeouts.

If the trend *really* is your friend—what is trading against the trend? How about this: Trading against the trend is like standing in front (financially speaking) of a speeding express train! So the next time you're contemplating taking a position or you are in one and are considering either closing it out or possibly adding to it, remember the realistic choice you have: With-the-trend = your friend; against the trend = standing in front of a speeding express train! Which would you choose?

CHAPTER NINE

Why Is the Speculator (Almost) Always Long?

I could hardly believe what I was hearing from the voice on the phone. We were talking about long-term trading systems, and the gentleman from South Dakota was bemoaning the fact that he had been continuously whipsawed in the Chicago grain markets throughout 1985. "I certainly hope we get some good grain trends in 1986," he went on, "because I can't take much more of these crazy, trendless markets." Crazy, trendless markets, I mused. What can he possibly be talking about?

Grains had been in a dynamic downtrend for nearly all of 1985—corn had declined from 2.85 in April to 2.20 by September. Wheat had slipped from 3.60 in March to 2.75 by July— and that's $4,250 per contract. And finally there were soybeans, which had absolutely astounded the Chicago bean-watchers by declining almost continuously since June of 1984 (see Figure 9–1). In fact, some of the astute systems traders, who had heeded the clear sell signal on the afternoon of June 11, 1984, were sitting with about $12,000 in open profits (per contract) on the short bean position. These ultimately closed out on December 16, 1985, with a $10,500 profit.

What the gentleman from South Dakota really meant—although he may not have realized it—was that he hoped the grain markets would turn *up*, simultaneously turning up his confidence factor, so that he could load up on the long side and make some money.

FIGURE 9–1   Long-Term Weekly (Nearest Future) Soybeans
Soybeans had been in a major bear market since mid-1984, on the failure of
the rally at the 9.00 level. Can you imagine a trader calling the market action
during 1985 trendless? It is about as classic a downtrend as you will ever see.
Astute position traders, who were willing to take a short position in an obvious
bear market, scored significant profits.

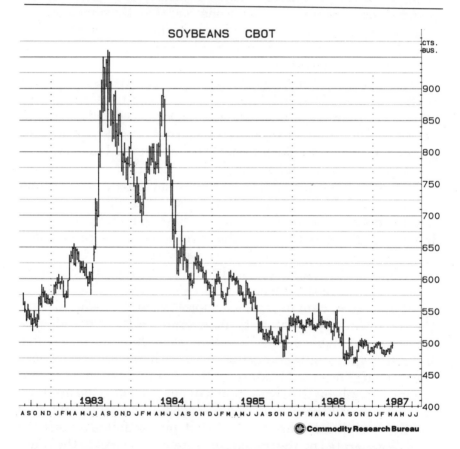

Have you ever noticed that when the average trader says that
a market is "good," he means that the trend is up *and* that he is
long? When he describes the market as "bad," he means that the
trend is down and that he is long. Long either way, it seems. But
here, he is stuck with a painful losing position in a clear-cut bear
market.

I suppose that it is human nature to look forward to advancing, rather than declining, prices and values. Since the end of

World War II, inflation has been steadily entrenched in the world economy, despite its apparent slowdown during the late 1980s. We have been convinced by the politicians and the media that inflation is healthy and desirable both for the economy and the individual. After all, who really wants to earn less in one year than he did the year before? Who wants the value of his house, property, or business to be less in one year than the previous one? One might even be accused of being antisocial or even un-American for anticipating or actually profiting from declining prices or economic values.

But politics and economic theory aside, the inescapable truth is that markets do trend down about half the time, that "they slide faster than they glide," and that experienced and successful operators know they can often achieve more reliable and quicker profits on the short side of a market than on the long side.

A major impediment to the average speculator catching significant down moves with any degree of consistency is his—and probably his broker's—innate bias for the long side of any market. Even when the trend is obviously down, our erstwhile speculator still clings to the hope that prices will reverse or, more specifically, that he will catch that reversal and make a big score. That has always been and will surely continue to be a most expensive speculative bias.

Rather than clinging to such subjective and hopeful visions, the responsible speculator should operate on the basis of some objective and viable approach—either something he has created himself, a service or market letter to which he subscribes or one of the computer-oriented trading systems now on the market. But having a viable method or system will not itself develop profits— it must be used the way it was intended, consistently and in a totally disciplined manner. And that means following *all* the signals generated by the method or system, and not just the "buy" signals or the ones that support the trader's personal biases.

I once wrote an article discussing the overwhelming penchant that traders have for the long side of the market, even in the face of an overall bearish price trend. A number of people wrote to me suggesting that this particular market bias was principally a public speculator's approach and that experienced operators would more realistically respond to bearish markets by placing their bets on the short side.

It's difficult to prove either point. How can you get a bunch of professional traders or analysts to divulge their real market positions? But, just such a glimpse becomes available twice yearly, in the guise of *The Wall Street Journal*'s semiannual survey of 20 leading commodity experts. The survey consists of buy and sell recommendations for the coming six months. The following ratings were made in January 1984 and are based on the experts' rankings, with three points given to a first choice, two points given to a second choice, and one point given to a third choice.

Buy foreign currencies	20 points
Buy T bonds	15 points
Buy stock indexes	15 points
Sell heating oil	12 points
Buy soybeans	10 points
Buy silver	7 points
Buy hogs	5 points
Sell soybeans	5 points

The results speak for themselves; six of the eight recommendations were buys, notwithstanding the fact that futures markets were generally forming a major top from which prices would be moving south for the next two-plus years. As a matter of fact, only two of the eight recommendations resulted in profits, and these were—can you guess?—the two lowest-rated recommendations: buy hogs and sell soybeans. If you tally the market performance of these eight "best bets" for the first half of 1984, you would find a most startling conclusion. The following calculations are based on a one-contract position in each market.

			Profit	Loss
Buy	Sept	D-mark		$ 1,000
Buy	Sept	Swiss		4,100
Buy	Sept	yen		1,562
Buy	Sept	T bond		2,587
Buy	Sept	S&P		8,875
Sell	Aug	heating oil		1,029
Buy	Aug	soybeans		2,650
Buy	Sept	silver		3,250
Buy	Aug	hogs	$ 981	
Sell	Aug	soybeans	2,650	
			$3,631	$25,053

Now, I do not suggest that someone would, in fact, have lost all that money. At some point in the slide, the trader would probably have closed out at least some of the losing positions and perhaps even have taken to the short side. Nevertheless, this summary bears ample witness to the fact that buy recommendations vastly outnumber sell recommendations regardless of the market and regardless of the operator's experience and sophistication. The same phenomenon is found among stock recommendations issued by brokerage firm analysts, where *buy* recommendations typically prevail over *sells* by nine to one!

The results of the summary also testify to the extreme difficulty (impossibility?) of attempting to predict the course of futures prices. Whereas, even an expert might be right on any given prediction, when you get down to a broad list of predictions, our expert is likely to bat far less than 50 percent. Another truth is self-evident here—reasonable stop protection is essential to prevent what could be just a modest and acceptable loss from deteriorating into a financial disaster.

Perhaps the longest-running bear show in recent memory was the foreign currency slide (the dollar bull market) that continued from 1978 through 1985. The Swiss franc declined from 69.00 to 35.00, the D-mark from 58.00 to 29.00, and the British pound from 2.40 to around 1.05. Notwithstanding this very long-term bear market, we have witnessed a near continuous round of bottom-picking, with both professional and commission house speculators chasing after the most elusive prize of all—the reversal of the strong dollar. There were probably more traders throughout the world watching and waiting for a bottom in currencies during much of that seven-year period than for any other future traded. The key questions traders had to face and will continue to face in similar situations in the future are these:

1. Were the currency markets forming a significant reversal from down to up at various times during the seven-year bear market?
2. How could the operator have participated in such a reversal while maintaining reasonable loss protection in the event, as actually occurred, the reversal signals were false and the market continued to decline?
3. Assuming the trader had reversed to long and had been stopped out, how could he have gotten back short in conformity with the ongoing bear trend?

I have often noted that major, long-standing trends, particularly downtrends, do not reverse very quickly. They generally take an intolerable amount of time and are accompanied by innumerable false signals that cause many operators to be whipsawed in and out to an exasperating degree. However, there is a logical way to shift the odds a bit more in your favor. Avoid trying to pick off tops and bottoms because, at best, it is a subjective and arbitrary way to time trades. Moreover, it hardly ever succeeds. Rather, you must exercise the patience and discipline to wait until your technical indicators or system tell you that the flip has occurred, at which point you should get aboard in the direction of the newly emerged trend. If your indicator reverses you, protect the new position with a reasonable stop. This could also be a reversal stop to return you into the ongoing trend if the reversal turns out to be false and untenable.

In the specific case of the currencies and their seven-year bear market, we discreetly avoided probing for the bottom so long as markets continued to slide within a broad succession of lower highs and lower lows. There was no logical way to form a sufficiently strong prediction of a market reversal on which to place a large bet. Overeager traders had been chopped up for years trying unsuccessfully to do just that. Instead, we approached these markets in the following manner: At each point where it appeared the market might be making a bottom (or a flip from short to long), we identified the respective resistance points. Each currency market would have to *close through* these in order to justify in our analysis that the trend had flipped. We had a number of close calls and "almosts," but as you can see from the accompanying long-term chart of the Swiss franc (Figure 9−2), the trend was clearly down. No rally high surpassed any previous rally high until first half of 1985, after the market hit bottom around the 34.00 level. One of the long-term trading systems we follow gave an initial buy signal on March 12, 1985, and a subsequent buy signal on June 13 of the same year. This analysis was further confirmed by our technical advisory, issued after the first rally from 34.00 to 41.00 and the subsequent *50 percent retracement* to the 37.00 level. It suggested the purchase of Swiss at 38.05 stop, *close only* (basis long-term weekly). We would wait to buy on the failure of the reaction *and* on the resumption of the rally.

Even after taking a position on a projected trend reversal, it is

---

FIGURE 9–2   Long-Term Monthly (Nearest Future) Swiss Franc
Here is the quintessential long-term roller-coaster market. The Swiss franc
topped out around the 69.00 level in late 1978, remaining within the major bear
trend until first-half 1985. This seven-year-long bear market was a near total
disaster for the majority of public speculators who were committed to the bull
side regardless of market trend. By the time the trend reversed to north in mid-
1985, most speculators missed the turn. They were too exhausted, both
financially and emotionally, from fighting the markets with their losing long
positions over the past several years. A number of public commodity funds,
however, scored impressive profits on short currency positions during this
period.

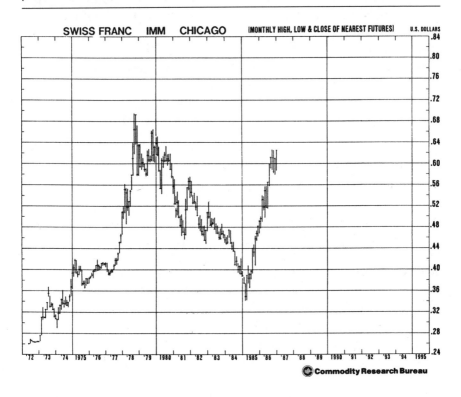

SWISS FRANC   IMM   CHICAGO   (MONTHLY HIGH, LOW & CLOSE OF NEAREST FUTURES)   U.S. DOLLARS

© Commodity Research Bureau

necessary to protect the new position with reasonable stops. So
what is reasonable? That is a function of the trader's personal
pain level. In my book, it can be set at anywhere from 50 to 100
percent of the margin requirement which, in actual dollar terms,
is from $600 to around $1,500. Obviously, how much you are
willing to risk is clearly related to how much you logically project
to win. So, if you are a very long-term operator with a history of

taking thousands from a winning long-term move, you can obviously afford a somewhat higher risk on a given position than a trader who is quicker to jump out.

We have all seen too many examples of antitrend trading. The same goes for top or bottom picking *against* major trending markets, where the operator loses—$15,000 or more per contract—all out of proportion to what he could reasonably have expected to win. And, as you can surmise, after taking a bath of that magnitude, he isn't likely to have much enthusiasm for getting back aboard when the market signals its next turn, even though this is just when he should be back in. But what if, instead of having lost several thousand per contract, he had lost under a thousand? He could then patiently wait for the next opportunity as signaled by his system or other technical method. He would again risk another thousand on the new position. Assuming his system or technical method was viable, he would ultimately score on the position, notwithstanding the few small losses along the way.

Remember the old children's rhyme, "He who fights and runs away lives to fight another day." I would dedicate to the speculator a revised version: "He who has a bad trade and runs away, lives to trade (and make profits) another day."

Have you ever tried to quantify the long-short mix of your portfolio versus the long-short mix of the actual market trends? I have, and the results were quite revealing. In May of 1985, I called several of my colleagues to inquire how they and their clients were positioned in the markets. I also called a number of overseas traders and money managers

Surprisingly, each of the individuals I called was willing to give me a frank rundown on his positions. Not surprisingly, nearly all the non-professional traders and far too many of the professionals were overwhelmingly long in the face of a particularly bearish environment where a clear predominance of markets was locked within strong downtrends. At the time, my trend analysis revealed the following breakdown:

1. *Uptrends*: coffee, heating oil, and soybean oil.
2. *Downtrends*: copper, D-mark, gold, lumber, soybean meal, sterling, sugar, Swiss franc, T bond, and yen.
3. *Sideways*: Corn, oats, platinum, S&P, silver, soybeans, T bills, and wheat (new crop).

A brief summary indicates that of the 21 markets under review, only 14 percent were uptrending, 48 percent were downtrending, and 38 percent were sideways—hardly the time for traders to be taking a predominantly bullish market stance. In fact, under these circumstances, a thoughtful market strategy would suggest a portfolio mix of not more than 15 to 25 percent on the long side.

However, this logical market strategy must be accompanied by the *patience* to allow your *with-the-trend* positions to fully develop for the full extent of the move. Patient long-term holding of with-the-trend positions is how the leading operators score the megaprofits. But patience is clearly a two-edged sword. Sitting patiently with an antitrend, losing position is a sure-fire ticket to big losses, a truism to which just about every trader can attest.

This discussion of market trends reminds me of an incident in Geneva in 1984. During a strategy session with a banker friend, I asked his opinion of a prominent "goldbug" who, for the past several years, had been doggedly predicting an imminent U.S. hyperinflation accompanied by a spectacular increase in the price of gold to $1,000 an ounce.

The goldbug's credentials were more impressive than his market acumen because events and trends in the real market were totally at odds with his extreme pronouncements. My banker friend pondered the question briefly. "See that clock on my mantle," he said. "It hasn't worked for years, yet it's right twice a day." The lesson was loud and clear: Don't ever allow yourself to become locked into an opinion or market position at variance with the *real* trend of the *real* market. You must believe and adapt to what is actually happening in the major trends of the real market. Ignore these major trends at your financial peril.

PART THREE

Timing of Trades

The Three Most Important Speculative Attributes: DISCIPLINE, DISCIPLINE, and DISCIPLINE

It was Wednesday, March 23, 1983. I had been restless the previous night, had awakened earlier than usual and got to the office by 8:30, positioning myself in front of the price screen and my various charts and studies. It was still a full two hours before the opening of the Chicago grain markets, but I could already feel the mounting excitement. Momentarily distracted by a ringing phone, I settled back to reexamine the soybean market and to review my strategy for the morning.

May beans had closed at 6.11 the previous day, and my market analysis, which I'd scribbled on a manilla card, read, "The trend in beans will not turn up until May can close or gap open above 6.23. I would be a buyer on either a close or a gap opening above that level. Following such a dynamic breakout, I would expect prices to soar."

The action of the past few sessions told me that the long-awaited bull breakout should be imminent, and a quick call to my Chicago floor man confirmed that the floor was looking for a sharply higher opening. That ought to do it! I entered my buy orders for the opening, sat back, took a deep breath, and waited for the first ticks on my little green screen (see Figure 10-1).

My opening gambit—putting on or adding to a position on a

FIGURE 10−1 May 1983 Soybeans
On the morning of March 23, the market gapped up through the 6.23 resistance level in a decisive show of strength. Following this impressive breakout, prices turned reactionary for three months, retracing some 50 percent of the previous up-leg. This brief price reaction proved to be the bears' final chance; the market then commenced a rally of monumental proportions. Three months later, the bull deal of 1983 was the big news in Chicago. The market had advanced by $3.75, equal to about $18,000 per contract. And that ain't hay, brother!

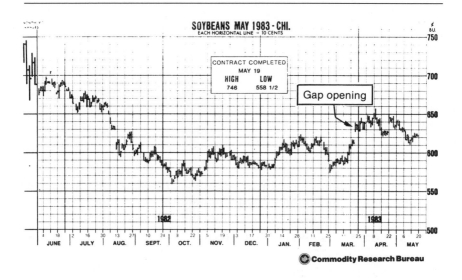

significant opening breakout gap—has been one of my favored tactics for many years. It is a risky but potentially valuable move for the aggressive operator. I endorse it primarily when the gap opening is in the direction of the ongoing major trend. As a secondary tactic, you can trade the gap opening when it represents a clear breakout from a broad sideways trading range that would either, *(a)* establish a major trend reversal or *(b)* constitute a continuation of an ongoing trend out of the lateral area. I would be very cautious about buying or selling gap openings that are clearly against the major ongoing trend because these gaps are often traps set up by trade or floor operators to "sucker" commission house speculators into untenable positions. Such brash anti-trend gap plays may look tempting, but they are best left to seasoned professionals who can run quickly if the trade starts to turn sour.

May beans had opened at 6.26½, closing the trap on the hapless bears. While waiting for my reports, my mind drifted back 10 years to the first time I had seen this opening gambit in action. My mentor in this art of trading on gap breakouts was Mike Green, a shrewd and aggressive Comex floor trader. As a new Comex member during the early 1970s, I frequently walked over to the exchange and down into the ring to study the pit action. I used to watch in awe as Mike Green, standing in the center of the copper crowd, his body and voice straining, would be buying at the opening . . . 50 lots . . . 100 lots . . . 150 lots at a clip. It was a bull market, and Mike knew it well. He seemed a master at waiting patiently until his well-honed instinct told him that each successive minor reaction had run its course and that the underlying bull trend was about to reassert itself. Then, and only then, did he spring into action—"buy 50 . . . buy 100 . . . buy 150."

Knowing when *not to trade*—patiently standing aside until just the right moment to enter the market—is one of the toughest challenges facing the trader. But it is essential if you are to stand in the winners circle. I have known countless days when the compulsion to overtrade was so strong that I had to resort to little ploys to keep myself from entering orders. These have included the following:

- Affixing a Livermore quote, "Money is made by sitting, not trading," to my order phone.
- Positioning a boating magazine atop my desk (that would normally suffice to take my mind off doing some unwarranted trades).
- In extreme cases, leaving the office for a brief walk or a bout with the flounder, blue fish, or whatever was then running in Manhasset Bay.

More often than I care to admit, I've closed out all or part of a winning position prematurely. Other times, I've just missed the move completely, then watched the action from the sidelines awaiting the next reaction to get back aboard. I once spent over a month stalking both copper and silver, having gained eight pounds snacking instead of trading (all in the line of duty) before reentering the market on a minor trend reversal. Despite all this, the simple truth remains: The successful trader maintains the discipline and objectivity to remain on the sidelines until he can enter the market in the direction of the major trend. Even then, you must be careful not to jump in on a random spurt when big orders from uninformed and weak speculative operators are thrown at the market. Even if you are trading in the trend direction, you'll need even more discipline and patience to sit through the inevitable price reaction created by the floor traders and commercial firms, designed to shake out the weak holders from their positions and as much of their bankrolls as possible.

It is too bad that futures trading tends to bring out the worst in most speculators. By and large, traders should perform better than their bottom-line results indicate. Their underperformance is principally attributable to their lack of discipline, and that inevitably leads to a lack of confidence. As a case in point, I recall a phone conversation I had with Dr. F. from San Diego, who told me that he had a long position in T bonds and wanted my opinion of what to do about it. I learned that he had been long for several weeks, from a much lower level, so that the position was showing a big paper profit. "Look," I countered, "why ask me what you should do with the position? You were smart enough to have gotten aboard near the beginning of the bull move and to have held on for the rise. Just follow the same instinct or the same technique, and you should be fine. Besides, "I mused, almost as an afterthought," I missed the long side of that bull market. After the surge breakout, I kept waiting for a 40 or 50 percent pullback, which didn't occur, and I never did get aboard."

In fact, Dr. F. had just been intimidated by a spate of contra-dic-tory information in the financial press during recent weeks. I diagnosed his current malady as ALOSC (Acute Lack of Self-Confidence). After a brief confidence-restoring pep talk, I pre-scribed a couple of days rest, a return to his drawing board for an objective analysis of the market, and a disciplined adherence to trend-following strategy.

And it isn't just commission house speculators or even profes-sional operators whose lack of effective discipline frequently stands between them and profitable trading results. Over the course of some 30 years, I've observed a curious anomaly between the market judgment of commodity producers and the eventual price action of their products. Invariably, producers tend to be more bullish than the market warrants. During the summer of

1983, I spoke with a number of midwestern corn farmers, whose crop outlook was dismal—reduced acreage, smaller yields, and stunted stalk growth. And who should know better about crop conditions than the people who actually grow the corn? All in all, a tremendously bullish situation, right? And clearly a golden opportunity for us speculators to get aboard and take advantage of the forthcoming crop disaster. Well, a funny thing happened to the long speculators on the way to the bank with their winnings— the market declined by 60 cents, a move of $3,000 per contract representing some six times the margin per contract. And if the (long) speculators were surprised at the market weakness, it was nothing compared to the amazement of the Midwest farmers, many of who were among the speculators who got killed on the long side of the corn market.

In fact, it seems commonplace for commodity producers, particularly growers of agricultural crops, to take an excessively bullish view of their market. This is due to crop or weather situations in their particular growing area, the hype from local politicians about how much better off they are going to be, or just plain wishful thinking. Unfortunately, when the crop is finally harvested and the serious hedge selling materializes, these bullish expectations often turn sour and prices head south.

There are times when widespread bullish expectations can substantially mesmerize an entire universe of producers; if the anticipated price advance actually turns into a price rout, the outcome for the producers can be devastating. The Maine potato market during the mid-1970s comes to mind—and it provides an object lesson in the need for discipline in any kind of market operation, be it speculative or trade hedging. It was a period of exuberant, uninhibited speculation in Maine potatoes on the New York Mercantile Exchange. Margins were low (you could trade for $200 margin per contract, or even less), and even memberships on the exchange were low (I bought my membership on the Merc for around $1,800). This environment allowed experienced growers, their bankers and brokers, all who should have known better to create the amazing strategy for which a special name was coined—the Texas Hedge.

As any college finance major knows, banks require as a precondition for providing farmers with financing on their growing crops, that the crop, or at least a substantial portion of it, be hedged. So the Maine potato farmers did just that—they hedged their crops on the exchange by buying huge amounts of April and May potato futures. BUYING futures? Hold on a minute—that doesn't sound quite right. If they are long the crop in the ground, aren't they supposed to hedge by SELLING futures? Yes, of course, *they should have sold.* (Oops!)

Just picture a lot of potato growers *buying* futures as a hedge. Some hedge! Of course, the commission house specs were also in there buying and adding to their big long positions to take advantage of the projected bull market that would make them all rich. So, since there has to be a seller for every buyer in a futures contract, who were all those dummies selling and going heavily short? Just the wealthy and experienced trade firms and professional operators, that's who.

The outcome should be readily predictable. Visualize an overcrowded rowboat, unstable to begin with, in which suddenly all the passengers jump to one side (the SELL side). And that's precisely what happened to the potato market, except that the big "splash" wasn't accompanied by a lot of salt water—it was a lot of red ink! The lesson was not lost on the commercial banks and big growers, who have since relearned the necessity of enforcing a strict and objective discipline into their hedging operations.

Another outcome that should be readily predictable is when a trader is holding two positions—and closes out a profitable with-the-trend position in order to free up margin to defend a losing antitrend position. But I'm getting a bit ahead of myself. Anyway, K. phoned me some time ago wanting to know what I thought of lumber. "Lumber," I repeated, "It's a terrific building material. You can build houses, boats, furniture . . . even carve those cute little toys and animal figures."

That wasn't really what K. wanted to know. What did I think of the lumber *market*? And what should he do with his big long position (of course, it was long *and* against the trend) on which he was now sitting with a $90,000 loss? I told him that whenever I think of trading lumber, I look for a nice comfortable place to lie down until the feeling passes. The market is too thin for my liking, it does not seem to trend reliably, and it is susceptible to distortion and excessive volatility. In short, I find the lumber market eminently resistible. As a matter of fact, my attitude regarding trading lumber should not have surprised him. It was the same admonition that I gave him, and which he completely ignored, *before* he got locked into this antitrend losing position. At that point, totally chagrined, K. confessed that he had just sold out his long November soybeans, on which he had a good profit in an excellent trending position, to defend (provide margin for) his losing lumber contracts. My advice to K. was very direct—close out the lumber and rebuy the beans.

His response was not unexpected—the lumber loss was now too big, and he would wait for a strong rally before liquidating. "How can I close out the lumber now, at this price?" he kept repeating. "That's easy," I responded. "You just pick up the phone, call your broker, and tell him to sell the entire lumber position *at the market*, that's how."

K. unfortunately stuck with the lumber position, neglecting my advice, which wasn't based on any brilliant market insight but on a time-tested and proven investment maxim—You keep what shows you a profit and close out what shows you a loss. Quite predictably, in the three-month interval following that conversation, the lumber position declined by another $27.00, while the closed-out soybean position advanced nearly $1.60. Had K. switched out of the lumber and back into the beans, he would have earned back his loss instead of sinking even deeper in the hole well beyond the initial $90,000 loss.

Human nature and our normal commercial instincts may be traders' worst enemy in this commodity trading game. Why is the speculator invariably looking to sell rallies in an uptrending market and to buy declines in a downtrending one when, time after time, the play results in big losses? Shortly after the conversation just related, I watched the November bean future, following a period of sharply rising prices, stage the singular most remarkable display I had ever seen. The market opened limit bid at 9.35, and, within a few hours, it plunged some 55 cents, equal to $2,750 per contract down to $8.80. In fact, during the session the market seesawed by 40 to 60 cents and, at one time, the ticks were coming in 3- to 5-cent increments. After the smoke had cleared and the market had actually closed UP 20 cents on the day, the losses to speculators caught in the vicious intraday swings totaled in the tens of millions. Why had the market swung so viciously? The postmortem revealed that an unusually large number of commission house speculators were playing "let's pick the top," hoping to find the precise moment to line up shorts before the market collapsed. In fact, the annals of futures trading are littered with the financial wreckage of "smart" traders who plunged (the wrong way) at false tops and bottoms. They sell rallies and buy declines for the simple reason that, in their impatient, irrational analysis, the market advanced or declined too far and too fast. There is also the trader who plunges against a fast-moving trend because he got prematurely suckered out of a good trending position and now, out of the market and watching it continue its move, he thirsts for "absolution" in the form of profits on the other side of the market.

Regrettably I too am something of an "expert" on this subject. Among my assortment of inexcusable plays, my soybean top-picking exercise stands out supreme. As a result, whenever I hear someone talking about taking on a position with the rationalization, "How much can I lose," I reply, "Pick a number. Make it a very big number. That's how much you can lose."

This play, in fact, occurred in the early 70s, but it is still fresh in my memory. Here is one of the universal gaffes that speculators commit. It was during the wild markets of 1972, and I had "caught" the bean market twice—first, when I bought May bean oil around 10.30 and sold it a few weeks later at 11.30. Not such a bad profit, I reasoned. It then continued its "little" advance all the way up to 17.00 . . . without me. Remember the old movie, *The Postman Always Rings Twice*? So apparently does the sucker-trader because shortly thereafter I bought May beans at 3.19, more at 3.22, and again at 3.24 (ok so far), closing out the entire position at 3.36—just before the market commenced its record-shattering bull advance!

Following my sale at 3.36, I watched the market reach the crazy, unheard of, and "unsustainable" price of 8.58, and I just "knew" that it was ripe for a good short sale. The price had exceeded my maximum upside "count," all technical indicators (*except for one*, which we'll get to shortly) shouted "overbought," and past bean bull markets had generally topped out during May or June. So-o-o, I put out a small short line in July beans around the 8.58 level, seemingly a (relatively) safe level to be short, and I resolved not to add to my short line until my initial position showed a good profit (at least, I did *something* right). I further determined not to overstay the market if it turned sour and to dump it if the short position proved a mistake. And that's exactly what happened, and that's exactly what I did. I covered the short position just two weeks later, *for a loss of $15,930 per contract*, shortly before the market topped out at, would you believe, 13.00.

This painful (and somewhat embarrassing) lesson should not be lost on you traders the next time you feel the urge to ignore your disciplined strategy, to revert to your wishful thinking fantasy mode, or to probe a dynamically trending market for anti-trend tops or bottoms. Oh yes, I mentioned that all technical indicators *except one* supported my bearish prognosis and my decision to short the beans. What was that? It was *that the trend was still up!*

In this discussion of the *discipline* needed for successful operations, I have thus far presented my own viewpoint on the basis of my own experiences. These have included being a Merrill Lynch account executive for four years, a market analyst for three, president and operating officer of a clearing firm for seven years, and a money manager for another handful of years. But despite having been a member of several exchanges for seven years, my only pit experience was *(a)* going down to the floor to observe trading and *(b)* once trying, but not succeeding, to fill a simple 50-lot copper switch on Comex. Therefore, I thought it might be of interest to present the viewpoints of some successful and able Chicago floor brokers concerning *discipline* in futures trading.

The *FIA Review* is the magazine of the Futures Industry Association and is available by subscription from the association.[1] The January/February 1987 issue presented a most interesting interview with four floor traders—"Floor Traders Talk About the Discipline Needed to Trade a Plan." Each of the four men interviewed works at a different specialty on the floor—one is a floor broker, filling orders for the account of other persons or firms; one is an arbitrageur who trades in spreads, seeking profits in the changing relationships between two different but related markets; one is a scalper, a very short-term player who helps provide liquidity on the floor and who rarely takes a position home overnight; and the fourth is a position trader who, by his own admission, "is looking for the big play, in long-term trends."

Here is what these gentlemen had to say about trading *discipline.*

---

[1]The Futures Industry Association, 1825 Eye Street NW, Washington, DC 20006

The arbitrageuer: "The most important thing that I have found over the nine years that I have been a member of the CBT is that, for the member to be successful . . . I don't think it is a fundamental understanding of the markets as much as it is a fundamental understanding of yourself. To be more specific, I am talking about *self-discipline*."

The scalper: "*Discipline* is the key to any kind of trading. I don't care if it is long-term speculating or tick-to-tick pure scalping. Trade by the rules. Take that quick loss. I've done it. We've all done it, I am going to buy something, and if it goes four ticks against me, I'm out. But it goes four ticks, so I watch it awhile (instead of getting out). And then the four turns into 40. Now, all of a sudden, from what was going to be a quick play, you're committed. The bottom line is that it takes *discipline* to follow the game plan."

The position trader: "A position trader has to be *disciplined* too. He's got to know when he enters a position where he's going to get out with his loss. A position trader generally is going to have a particular loss that he is willing to accept up front like the scalper will. He's got to be *disciplined*. He's got to sit there and see the market go against him and say, I'm not getting out because I am right. But he's got to have a stop when he knows he's wrong. The market is always right. You're not always right. As a position trader, I recommend putting in paper stops [SK—he means actually entering the stop orders, not using so-called mental stops]. The *discipline* is to have it in there; I always put my stops on paper, and that way I know I'm out. Then I'm out and I take another look at the market and make another decision whether I want to get back in or not."

The floor broker: "The floor broker must *discipline* himself to know what the technical trader is likely to do at specific price levels and where are the support and resistance levels in each of his markets. He can't get caught up in the excitement of the moment and must know what effect various types of news will have on the market and its trends."

In summary, regardless of what you choose to trade and how you choose to trade it, these experienced floor brokers recommend that you have a plan. It must include a bail-out point to keep your losses under control. And, of absolute importance, you must have the *discipline* to stick to your plan.

_____

CHAPTER ELEVEN

Market Action Invariably Discounts the News

Some years ago, I was collaborating with an economic analyst on a cocoa report. This was before I had reached the conclusion that cocoa was, from a long-term trader's point of view, untradable, and that the appropriate way to deal with the stuff was to eat it, not trade it. Anyway, my colleague and I got onto the subject of news versus price action. He was nonplussed when I advanced the theory that more often the price makes the news, rather than vice versa. "Ridiculous," he bellowed. "It's common knowledge that the price reacts to the news, period." I'm not generally a betting man, but I'm always willing to put some money down against the "common knowledge" theory of the universe. So the bet was duly made, with my thesis being that I could reasonably predict the news by watching the price and its interaction with the other technical factors in the market. It was the easiest $20 I ever made.

We were in the midst of a fairly strong bull trend, with the long side held largely by (weak) commission house specs and the short side primarily by trade firms and a few professional trading houses. (As you can guess, I had my own private theory as to who was going to win this one.) Following the first sharp break (the explanation for the big moves generally comes out after the fact),

I postulated that the forthcoming news would be either:

1. One of the producing nations had suddenly "discovered" that they had more cocoa for export than they had previously (on the last rally, no doubt) announced.
2. A large quantity of cocoa bags would be unexpectedly "discovered" in a cocoa warehouse in Philadelphia or New York.

It turned out to be the "Philadelphia warehouse discovery" story this time around. Score one for the home team. Following a barrage of speculative long liquidation on resting stops, the market recommenced its upward course. Many of the former trade and professional shorts had covered and jumped over to the long side on the recent reaction. We then had a vicious weeklong rally, including two limit-bid sessions, during which the trade firms were back in there on the sell side. Towards the end of that week, I notified my partner that the rally would be attributed to either:

1. The sudden and unexpected outbreak of black pod disease in an African growing region.
2. The sudden discovery that the capsid bug had done foul things to stored cocoa in U. S. East Coast warehouses.

It turned out to be the capsid bug story this time.

The sugar market provides an excellent glimpse at the unique relationship between price and market news. The way news is released *after* every move should be studied by every thoughtful trader. During an extended bear market in sugar, culminating around the 2.50 cent level in mid-1985, the decline was accompanied by every type of bearish news imaginable. But after the market had reversed and started moving north, the bearish news items were put back in the desk drawer, and suddenly the bullish items were trotted out for dissemination. On January 26, 1987, *following* a 200-point sugar rally (equal to $2,240 per contract on a $600 margin), *The Wall Street Journal* noted the following:

> Reports that the Soviet Union had been a large buyer of refined sugar in the world market helped futures to extend their advance, with the March contract closing at 8.22, up 22 points. Analysts said Moscow bought 500,000 to 700,000 metric tons of raw sugar . . . and one analyst said the Soviets may buy as much as a million tons more. Analysts said prices also were buoyed by a report that Brazil

will push back contracts to export 750,000 to 1.5 million tons of raw sugar to 1988 or 1989 and by reports that Cuba is having problems harvesting and milling its cane sugar crop. In Brazil, diversion of sugar to alcohol production, stronger domestic consumption, and indications that drought may reduce the crop have created tight supplies, analysts said.

They seem to have "trotted out" every bullish item they could think of, but following the first 200-point decline, you can bet that the news will "suddenly" become totally bearish.

And so it goes. The salient points to keep firmly in mind are that market prices fluctuate and that, *following every price move*, analysts and commentators are in there offering perfectly plausible explanations for *what just happened* in the market. To many thoughtful observers, all this so-called news, pit gossip, and rumor seem rather conveniently contrived by some of the professional and trade operators to confuse, confound, and generally sucker as many gullible traders as possible into untenable market positions.

There ought to be a way to avoid being caught in this recurring trap—and there is. As simplistic as this may sound, the astute trader just ignores the plethora of rumor, pit gossip, and what generally passes for market news. He maintains his focus on the real technical factors underlying each market and on whatever disciplined strategy has worked best for him and his particular style. He never loses sight of the old Wall Street maxim, Those that know, don't tell; those that tell, don't know.

Late in 1984, I had an interesting telephone conversation with a trader in Houston. How, he asked, could we be experiencing a bear market in corn with this year's crop roughly half the size of last year's? Answering that question, I came to grips once again with the frequent disparity between the price action of a given market and the fundamentals—or *perception* of those fundamentals. In fact, as we observe time and again, price is the significant equalizer between supply and demand and is the key factor that brings out the news and gossip of what *happened* (note past tense) in the market.

Back to the corn market. Sure, the recently harvested corn crop was considerably smaller than the trade and brokerage communities had projected at the beginning of the season, but the situation must be viewed in the context of price movements over the entire past year. In early 1983, corn was priced around 2.75 (nearest future) and, on the basis of the bullish fundamentals, rallied some 45 cents to 3.20 by April. Then, following a brief 20 cent bout of profit taking (just under a 50 percent reaction) the bull reasserted itself, with the market advancing to 3.75 by August. This $1 rally took just six months, and, least you be unimpressed with the move, it amounted to $5,000 per contract on a margin of just $700.

A bull market? Sure. But, in fact, the entire bull deal had already lasted a full year. By the time the price had reached the 3.75 level, the advance had discounted all the bullish news, and the trade and professional firms were then focusing on more sobering and less bullish factors, including a likely reduction in exports and the probability of a larger new crop. Well, was it still a bull market? Probably not! But it used to be one, before the price advanced, discounting the bullish factors. How was one to know?

Clearly, bullish and bearish market psychology exerts a major influence on traders' decisions to buy or sell. Experienced operators know that the price functions as a barometer: It discounts the future. But that's as far as it goes—you just can't get it to discount the hereafter. Where does that leave the trader? He watches the market, keeps his charts, reads the financial columns, subscribes to services or advisory letters, and hears market opinions from his broker and friends. That's a considerable volume of diverse information, and much of it is contrary and contradictory. So, how does the trader base his market decision on trend, support and resistance, price objective, stop-loss point, whether to pyramid, and so on? Lots of questions, with the bottom line being the single basic decision of buy, sell, or stand aside.

I think the answer is obvious—it has been stated here in previous sections and will be restated. Market action (prices) invariably discounts the news, and you can't be sure if the news is true or false. Even if it is true, has the market price already reacted to the news? And, further, even if you know the news to be true and know that the price hasn't yet reacted to it, that still leaves a lot of questions unanswered: how to limit risks, where to put stops, whether or not to add to the position, etc. These all lead back to the same conclusion. For success in market trading, you must focus on two areas:

1. A technical approach that has proven itself or possibly a

long-term trading system—most likely run on a computer—you have confidence in.
2. Sound trading strategy and the discipline to properly utilize this strategy.

Even a cursory examination of the long-term (weekly) corn chart (Figure 11–1) makes it obvious that the market topped out around the 3.75 level in mid-1983. But, as they say, hindsight has 20-20 vision. How would the trader have known this was a top? He couldn't have known at the time. Until the failure of the rally around the 3.62 level, in second-quarter 1984, the market still looked like a bull trend undergoing a normal technical correction. The failure of the rally against this 3.62 level was confirmation of the top. The relevant question remains—how should a trader have played this situation? More precisely, when and where would he have gotten short? In truth, you would probably get as many answers to that question as the number of people you asked. It might be of interest to examine exactly what signals were given by one of the long-term computer systems during that period (prices basis 91-day perpetual).

	Bought	Sold	Profit	Loss
A.	Mar 22, 1985 @ 278.8	May 01, 1984 @ 336.5	$2,825	
B.	Mar 22, 1985 @ 278.8	May 15, 1985 @ 273.9		$305
C.	Oct 31, 1985 @ 234.7	May 15, 1985 @ 273.9	1,900	

These three trades covered the 18 months from May 1, 1984, through October 31, 1985. Analyzing them in terms of trend and holding period, trade A was the initial short trade signaled as the market emerged from its major top area on May 1, 1984. This short position was held just under 10 months, with the system's trailing stop following the market down. The stop was touched off on the rally of March 22, 1985, and the position was covered and switched to long (trade B). The firmness proved to be temporary (although one had no way of knowing this at the time the short was covered). When the downtrend reasserted itself, the sell stop once again did its job, closing out the long position and reentering short (trade C), which was held for 5½ months. The profits and losses as well as the length of holding periods speak for themselves.

Perhaps some trader can come up with better results by fol-

FIGURE 11–1   Long-Term Weekly (Nearest Future) Corn
From a long-term perspective, corn actually topped out at the 3.75 level in
mid-1983, but we had no way of knowing this was the reversal. Actually, the top
was confirmed on the failure of the rally against the 3.62 level in mid-1984.
For the next two years, it was a bear trend, punctuated with occasional minor-
trend rallies. The long-term computer systems began signaling sell on
May 1,1984.

Weekly High, Low & Close of Nearest Futures

lowing the so-called news, pit gossip, and fundamental statis-
tics—but, I've never seen it happen, at least not on any sort of
consistent basis, and I won't believe it until I see it.

No discussion of market action versus market price can be
complete without some reference to El Nino.[1] As all you soybean
watchers know, El Nino is a powerful, periodic current of warm

---

[1]The literal translation from the Spanish is "the little boy." For a little boy,
he sure throws his weight around.

water that flows southward along the coast of Peru and can disrupt the normal weather in that part of the Pacific. In altering the ocean temperature along the Peruvian coast, El Nino can kill or drive away marine life and, in this respect, can directly affect the size of the Peruvian anchovy catch. So, what have anchovies got to do with soybean prices on the Board of Trade? Just this—anchovy is the principal ingredient in fish meal, which is a principal competitor of soybean meal in world markets.

If this is beginning to sound a bit fishy, just talk to any soybean analyst. He'll probably offer an involved and geographic or climate-oriented explanation about where and when El Nino will next strike, sending world soybean prices either soaring or reeling (meal and oil will be affected as well).

I have seen lengthy and intricate written studies concerning El Nino, most of which were far too involved to be meaningful to traders. So I have devised my own simple and direct technique for forecasting the presence or absence of EN in any given year.

I have eschewed any use or reference to climate analysis, histograms, or meteorological observations in my analysis. On what basis, then, do I set up my forecast for EN? I do it on the basis of price action, and here's how. Referring to the long-term monthly soybean chart (Figure 11−2), the market has generally fluctuated within the range of $4.00 to $10.00 over the past 15 years. Any time the market is in the upper portion of that range, say above $8.00, you can count on EN to be in action (or at least, *they'll say* EN is in action). Any time the market is in the lower portion of this broad range, say under $5.50, EN will be nowhere in evidence. From its base area, a nearest-month close over $6.50 would be quite bullish, and would undoubtedly be accompanied by authoritative predictions for an EN of significant proportions. Conversely, following a big bull market into the $9.00 or higher level, a nearest-month close below $7.50 would likely be the cue for EN to scoot off somewhere else in the vast Pacific, leaving the anchovy crop to multiply and prosper. This would undermine the price of fishmeal and ultimately soybeans via the reverse process.

By the way, if you have never witnessed the floor action on the Chicago Board of Trade during a bona fide soybean bull market, you have a real experience to look forward to.[2] A bull market in

---

[2]A bull market in soybeans is generally not confirmed until the market can advance out of its base and surpass the 6.50−7.00 level.

FIGURE 11−2 Long-Term Monthly (Nearest Future) Soybeans
With its vast public and professional participation, the soybean market creates
more instant millionaires with every bull market than any other bull or bear
market in any commodity. The ingredients for a big bull market exist any
time the market gets below 5.50 and subsequently rallies above 6.50 on a
closing basis. The price creates the news, with bullish news and gossip on
the rallies and bearish news and gossip on the reactions.

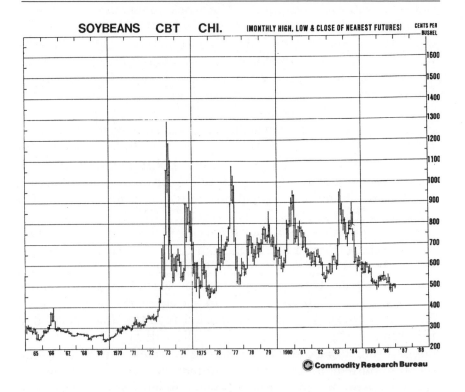

© Commodity Research Bureau

beans is the granddaddy of all bull markets. It is well worth your
trip to Chicago to watch the pyrotechnics from the gallery. Your
broker might even be able to arrange for you to tour the floor
while you are there. Incidentally, if (or when) we do get such a
soybean bull market, you'll undoubtedly see me, from time to
time, either in the gallery or down on the floor watching the
powerful frenzy as if for the first time—although, in truth, I've
been down there quite a bit more often than that. It's there on the
floor and in the pit action that you'll learn another side of the real
story of futures speculation.

CHAPTER TWELVE

Everyone Has a System

If you had scrutinized the apparel of the gentleman sitting alongside my desk a number of years ago—the one trading his head off in beans—you would have noticed something distinctly curious. The guy always wore a brown necktie—which may not have been so unusual, but it was always the same brown necktie. Since he was otherwise elegantly dressed, you might well have asked, Why the same brown necktie every day?

His answer was simple: The brown necktie was his Soybean Trading System. His Soybean Trading System? Exactly so—and for a period of several months, this otherwise intelligent and perfectly rational gentleman, this corporate officer of a major drug company, was totally convinced that his Soybean Trading System actually worked.

The guy—let's call him Marvin—had never actually traded commodities before, but at his club he overheard two "experienced traders" exchanging bullish gossip about soybean futures. That was all he needed to hear. The very next day, he walked up to the Merrill Lynch office where I was a freshman account executive, asked for a broker who knew how to read the commodity board (that turned out to be me), and opened his account. After I showed him how to read the grain prices on the big commodity board (these were the days before desk-top screens) plus some requisite logistics such as hours of trading, size of contracts, commissions, margins, and margin calls, he plunked down a check for $5,000 and plunged into 10M bushels (two contracts) of May soybean futures. But then, the most implausible and remarkable thing happened. He somehow lucked into the exact beginning of the renowned 1961 soybean bull market. We all watched incredulously as this total neophyte actually lurched from 10M to 225M beans (from 2 to 45 contracts) and from $10,000 to over $80,000 in equity.

And so it happened. The bean market had been limit down for three consecutive sessions (it was just a 10 cent limit back then). Marvin was losing $22,500 per day—probably half a year's pay—and he was feeling the hot breath of the margin clerk breathing down his back. Then he appeared in our office sporting his good luck necktie. It had become his good luck necktie when he once came from behind to win a big bridge tournament while wearing it. As luck would have it (although you could never get him to concede it was due to luck), after having been locked limit-down since the opening, the market staged a prodigious rally in the final 15 minutes of the session. It soared from limit-down to unchanged to, would you believe, LIMIT-UP. That evening Marvin treated himself, good luck necktie and all, to his first limo ride, from our midtown office to his apartment in the Bronx. Needless to say, from that day forward, regardless of whatever else he wore, his good luck brown necktie invariably encircled his freely perspiring neck. A curious trading system to be sure, but he was absolutely convinced that it worked, and that's what really counted for him. Regrettably, it stopped working shortly after his equity surpassed the $80,000 mark, but that's a different story altogether.

What isn't a different story is that we now live in an advanced, technological world, so that our trading systems can depend more on logic, mathematics, and computer programs than on good luck brown neckties.

At the forefront of this technology is the current crop of powerful microcomputers. In lightning speed, they can do studies and calculations that would have been unthinkable just a few years ago.

Everywhere I go and in just about every phone conversation and piece of correspondence, the focus seems to revolve around computer systems, software, on-line quotes, tick-by-tick charts, and so forth. The computer allows even the neophyte trader, after minimum hours studying the workings of the equipment and the operation of the software, to begin testing existing systems and to develop some of his own. He can combine interesting segments of different systems and try to come out with something that will fulfill his needs; that is, assist him in profiting from his trading activities—winning more on profitable positions, losing less on adverse ones.

So now, everyone has some sort of trading system. But was this always so? Here's some commentary about speculation and trading systems that I came across recently:

> The reader ought to thoroughly understand, however, that there is no royal road to speculation. Given all the conditions of the problem, and profits could be ciphered out with the accuracy of a mathematical demonstration. But the unknown quantities are the stumbling blocks of system mongers . . . Successful operators . . . cannot explain, even to themselves, yet they know when a stock is a good purchase, and when its price is running too high. None of them would allow that a system is possible, or could perfect their combinations, except by an unconscious use of this very impossibility.
>
> How easy it would be to fill a book with these figures! The charts teem with them. There is not a stock . . . which does not indicate . . . alternations of hope and fear in wide percentages and with unbounded opportunities for speculators to buy with confidence of profit. Brokers tell us that about one in a hundred buy in this manner. The 99 mean to do so. They make their calculations, add up, subtract, wander hither and thither for points, try this system and that theory, are wise to the extent of their wisdom, and come forth from their ventures shorn of all their golden fleece.

Do these words sound familiar to you? Have you read it in some Wall Street book or in one of the market advisories? You may have read something similar to this but, as Alphonse Karr once said, "The more things change, the more they remain the same." In fact, it's not likely that you've read this particular Wall Street quote recently—it was written by James K. Medbury in 1870.[1]

If traders were experimenting with systems back in the last century, they are more than ever doing it in the current one. In

---

[1]James K. Medbury, *Men and Mysteries of Wall Street* (Burlington, Vt.: Fraser Publishing, 1870, reprint 1968).

fact, it is probably true that just about every serious trader has, at one time or another, experimented with some type of trading system to improve the timing of trade entries, keep himself in a profitable position longer, or get out of a losing position sooner. All three of these objectives are important, and overall dollar success largely depends on the trader being able to pursue and attain these objectives.

The universal appeal of a good long-term, trend-following system is that positions are generally established in the direction of the trend reasonably near the onset of the move. A good system tends to keep you in the position so long as the market continues to move favorably and to stop you out, possibly reversing as well, when the trend reverses. The rub here lies in the phrase, "tends to keep you in the position" because, as all systems traders have discovered, it is frustratingly difficult to fine tune the market stops to stay aboard so long as the market is moving favorably, but (and this is the key "but") to stop and possibly reverse at just the right moment. In the real world of tension-filled, white-knuckled trading, stop placement will be an imperfect art at best. The stop will either be too close—and you will keep getting whipsawed on minor technical corrections—or too far—and you end up taking whopping big losses or else giving back most of your paper profits when the trend reverses. The solution to the problem of fine tuning the stops is probably the toughest part of successful systems design and is clearly the area that receives the maximum focus in new research and studies.

Another major problem with trend-following systems is that, during periods of broad sideways price movement—and these are far more prevalent than established, dynamic trends—the system follower is invariably buying on rallies and selling on reactions. These whipsaw losses are an inevitable part of trend-following trading. The operator needs have the patience and financial stamina to sit through a succession of whipsaw losses while waiting for the big move that will provide the big profits. It takes considerable patience and discipline to stick with a system that is broadly whipsawing you in and out of positions. However, our experience has shown that, once you have embarked on a viable trend-following approach, you will do far better sticking with it and following it to the letter than trying to second-guess and "improve" it.

As trading systems go, the moving average approach is clearly the oldest and most basic of all methods. In its simplest form, a moving average (m.a.) is the sum of X consecutive closes divided by X. For example, you obtain a nine-day simple m.a. by adding the closing prices for the last nine days and dividing the sum by nine. Perhaps the most popular simple m.a. combinations are the 5- versus 20-day, and the 4- versus 9- versus 18-day.

The "versus" enters the picture because traders have discovered through years of trial, error, and testing that a "crossover" technique captures the maximum advantage of a moving average. There are, essentially, two ways to play these simple systems, and they can amaze traders by sometimes outperforming more complicated and elaborate ones. You can take trades when the closing price crosses your m.a. line; for example, using a 19-day approach, you would buy when the price closes above the 19-day m.a. and sell (possibly reversing as well) when the price closes below the 19-day m.a. This simple system, however, offers less flexibility than the second approach, which uses a dual crossover; for example, a 5 – 20-day crossover, where you buy when the short-term line (the 5-day) closes above the long-term line (20-day) and liquidate the long, and go short as well, when the 5-day line closes below the 20-day.[2]

These basic strategies will surely get you aboard early in the trend, but you will just as surely encounter lots of premature moves coupled with whipsaw stop losses. However, the payoff arrives when the system gets you and keeps you in a position for an extended move.

Serious systems traders tend to get considerably more involved with moving averages. Some use so-called *weighted* moving averages, which give greater importance to recent than to older price action. For example, a 15-day weighted average might factor the most recent close at 15, the previous day at 14, and so forth, till you get to the oldest of the 15 days, which would be factored at 1. Then you would multiply the most recent close by its factor (15), the previous close by 14, and so forth, dividing the sum by the total of the factors, 120 in this case, in order to get the pertinent average. Other operators utilize exponentially smoothed

---

[2]In the 4 – 9 – 18-day strategy, you close longs when the 4-day closes below the 9-day, go short when the 9-day closes below the 18-day, and so forth.

averages, which incorporate a potentially infinite time span via more complex calculations. Such approaches clearly require the use of a sophisticated calculator or, as a more practical arrangement, a computer with customized software.

For any moving average system—regardless of its complexity—a critical question concerns the number of days in your average and whether it should be optimized (tailored) to each distinct commodity. In this regard, some of the best technical research has been done by technical analysts Frank Hochheimer and Dave Barker. Hochheimer tested a broad array of averages, from 3 to 70 days, on each of 13 different futures for the 1970–76 period. His results clearly indicated that there was no single "best" universal combination. His best *simple* moving average (closing price going through a moving average value), which projected best profits, looks like this:

	Best Average	Cumulative Profit/Loss	Number of Trades	Number of Profits	Number of Losses	Ratio Profits/ Total Trades
Silver	19 days	$ 42,920+	1,393	429	964	.308
Pork bellies	19 days	97,925+	774	281	493	.363
Corn	43 days	24,646+	565	126	439	.223
Cocoa	54 days	87,957+	600	157	443	.262
Soybeans	55 days	222,195+	728	151	577	.207
Copper	59 days	165,143+	432	158	274	.366
Sugar	60 days	270,402+	492	99	393	.201

Please note that these are hypothetical trades, done on the basis of an after-the-fact calculation. Real-time results are unlikely to show such profits. Also note the low ratio of profits to total trades, from .201 to .366—typical of systems and formula trading. Hochheimer went on to test the best combinations of linearly weighted moving averages, exponentially smoothed moving averages, and finally simple versus exponentially smoothed versus linearly weighted moving averages. The results of this research have been published in the 1978 Commodity Year Book (Commodity Research Bureau, New York).

For those traders interested in going beyond the simple, closing price versus a single moving average crossover, the dual moving average crossover approach would be the next step. With this technique, you calculate both a short- and a long-term moving average, say an 8- and a 35-day average. You would buy when the 8-day crossed above the 35-day and sell when the reverse occurred. Here again, Hochheimer did some excellent research in the testing of optimum crossover periods, using 20 different commodities for the years 1970–79. Some of his optimum combinations are:

Silver	13 versus 26 days
Pork bellies	25 versus 46 days
Corn	12 versus 48 days
Cocoa	14 versus 47 days
Soybeans	20 versus 45 days
Copper	17 versus 32 days
Sugar	6 versus 50 days

Another analyst who did some fine work in systems testing was Dave Barker, who tested the 5-and-20-day dual m.a. crossover system (without optimization) versus an optimized dual m.a. crossover system for the 1975–80 period. Not surprisingly, the optimized version consistently outperformed the straight 5-and-20-day version, and a partial list of Barker's best combinations follows:

Silver	16 versus 25 days
Pork bellies	13 versus 55 days
Corn	14 versus 67 days
Cocoa	14 versus 38 days
Soybeans	23 versus 41 days
Copper	4 versus 20 days
Sugar	14 versus 64 days

There are lots of other ways to use moving averages, some of them focusing on the momentum of the move. A London-based currency analyst of my acquaintance uses moving averages to both identify trends and to time trades. His overall focus is quite long-term, utilizing one-month (21-day) and three-month (63-day) averages in his technical work. As a start, he compares daily the price of the 21-day m.a. versus the price of the respective future 63 days ago, getting a sense of the momentum of the recent move. Then he examines the slope of the 63-day m.a., discerning a buy signal when the curve changes slope from down to up and a sell signal when the opposite occurs. Because this is quite a long-term approach, there are relatively few trades. This analyst told me that he made just five D-mark trades in 3½ years and claimed that his overall results were profitable. I've spoken to other analysts as well, many of whom went beyond moving average crossover analysis, focused instead on the slope of the m.a. lines, and took their signals on the change in slope of their various lines. However, I have not seen any real-time results from these methods.

These few studies were conducted during the 1970s and early 80s, and, clearly, a considerable amount of much more sophisticated research and testing has been done since that time. Nevertheless, these basic studies can help technically oriented operators as a starting point for the research and testing of more advanced and personalized trading systems.

A recurring thesis of mine is that a good technical method or trading system is only half of what is needed for overall successful operations. The other half—and of equal importance—is a viable strategy for applying the technical method or system. I would rather have a mediocre system coupled with an excellent strategy than an excellent system with mediocre strategy. The ideal solution, of course, would be a first-class system *plus* a first-class strategy.

Some time ago, I collaborated with a talented mathematician who had designed the parameters for an excellent computer-oriented trading system. During a lull in the technical aspects of our meeting, I asked for his thoughts on how a trader should approach a trading system in order to derive the maximum benefits from using it. Here was his list.

- He must have confidence in the system so he is not constantly trying to override, second-guess, or "improve" it on the basis of personal emotions, biases, or just plain wishful thinking.
- He must have the patience to wait on the sidelines for trading signals and then, once in a position, further patience to sit with it until a reversal signal is given.
- He must have the discipline to trade in accordance with both the signals and the trading strategy of his system.

Over the years I have had lots of correspondence with traders; many are experienced operators who have experimented with a succession of systems. The comments come as close to a universal experience in the use of trading systems as I've ever seen. Some contain excellent advice.

From S. H. in Redwood City, California:

I am very pleased with the system I am now using. For me, it comfortably and satisfactorily gives me guidance, is providing very good results, and is answering my problems with stop management and related profits or lack thereof. Had I not been using the system, my profits would have been greatly reduced.

From T. A. in Paris, France:

It unfortunately has taken me eight months to fully appreciate and accept everything the system comes up with. I've managed in spite of myself to make money, but I would have made considerably more had I not tried to find shortcuts within the system.

To be fair, I also had a lot to learn in the basics of trading commodities. I also had to learn a lot about myself—lack of patience, lack of discipline, general stupidity at times, and a desire to feel that I was capable of independent thought and not just a blind follower of someone else's system. What was amazing last year was that every time I went against the system, I lost. Not even the law of averages offered me a helping hand. I'm thankful that cotton and coffee made their magnificent moves to save me from myself.

Needless to say, in 1987, I will be following to the letter the buy and sell signals generated by the system. My tinkering to get an extra 5 – 10 points here and there has definitely not paid off. I've also come to the conclusion that I am as incapable as the next person of picking the tops and bottoms. Last year was excellent in one respect in that the pain of experience and suffering has burned in some very helpful lessons that I will not soon forget.

From M. L. in Austin, Texas:

I thought you might be interested in my three years of actual operating experience with the XYZ System. I purchased the system in May of 1983 and paper traded part of that year, since I found that I would, all too frequently, try to second-guess the system either by taking some trades and not others or by trying to anticipate trades. Quite honestly, little by little, I came to use the system the way it was intended, taking and then following the trading signals consistently and confidently.

The summation is that I started with $19,000 in my account and after three years I stood at $81,814. All this, in a consistent and reasonable progression, taking moderate risks and low drawdown.

As an extra bonus, the system teaches patience, consistency, diversification, and discipline. And, although the human emotions of greed and fear, which cause most speculators to accept small profits and large losses, are still part of the trader's universe, the system overcomes these impediments to profitable trading by helping the trader control these hangups and focus his trading into a disciplined and strategically viable speculation.

So what is the bottom line—that a computerized trading system is the best way to go? My answer is a resounding definitely . . . maybe. First of all, how good is the system? In my discussion of trading systems, I invariably qualify the subject with the adjectives, good, sound, and viable. But what is good, sound, and viable? And, even if you can specify and define them, how can you determine if a given system is good, sound, and viable? Perhaps the ultimate test would be a free, no-obligation trial period (and it's not likely that any system would be offered this way). But even that has its shortcomings. Results over any brief period may not be representative of its long-term capabilities. The best test would be to examine real-time trading results from traders who have actually been using the system for a period of at least two years—and you want to talk to as many different people as possible. Secondly, even if it is a successful system, you want to be sure that it is consistent with your trading approach and objectives. I have seen a trader spend substantial dollars on an excellent and proven system only to find it inconsistent with his trading approach (a long-term position system with a short-term trader). The system, regrettably, ended up on the shelf. In short, every system has its own personality and rationale, generally mirroring the personality and investment rationale of its developer, and though it may be a fine and viable system, it may not be the right one for you.

In considering a system, you must determine if it actually performs as the seller or the advertising literature claims. It often does not, to everyone's surprise. Some years ago, I met a trader from Seattle who was promoting a system that he had developed. He had excellent credentials and was associated with a reputable firm, so I decided to look into it further and was promised full cooperation. I asked for some real-time trading results and was shown trading records from the developer's own account, which were profitable and which tended to verify the system's claims. I was put off, however, in that they didn't show me real-time results with any other accounts. If it was such a good system, wouldn't other clients of the firm have come aboard? The next step in my due diligence inquiry was to monitor the signals daily, and I asked the developer to phone me with all signals as they were processed from the computer. Six weeks later, I decided that I had seen enough and dropped the inquiry. What put me off was not that nearly every trade during the entire six-week period was closed at a loss—that could be due to hitting a sideways nontrending market period. I was disturbed by something quite different. The system had been promoted as a long-term position approach, and, indeed, the historical paper trading record supported this claim. Regrettably, however, the signals phoned to me as they came forth from the computer seemed to have come from an altogether different system. Here is what I found:

- Paper trading showed 83 percent of all trades profitable; real-time trading showed just 12 percent of all trades profitable.
- Paper trading showed an average holding period of 34 days; real-time trading showed an average holding period of 5 days.
- Paper trading showed an average profit of $2,884; real-time trading showed an average profit of $440.

Needless to say, I have neither seen nor heard of this system since.

Another aspect of a computerized trading system that concerns traders is its cost, which can run anywhere from $75 to $7,500. In fact, the initial cost of a system may be the least relevant factor in the trader's decision. The most expensive system may turn out to be the most economical.[3] In selecting a trading system, price should be less relevant than performance (no—consistent performance), reasonable drawdown, a favorable

---

[3]This reasoning doesn't just apply to trading systems. The most economical automobile I ever owned was a three-year-old Rolls I bought from a New York dealer for $24,500. After four years of enjoyable use, I sold it for $25,000.

ratio between dollar profits and losses (a minimum of 3 to 1), and a compatible investment rationale.

I am skeptical of the so-called black box type of system, where trading signals pop out of a computer without the system providing some logical rationale or glimpse of the charts and relevant "lines" underlying the analysis. The trader ought to understand what his system is doing, why the signals say what they do, and what the lines look like. Naturally the precise formulation of the system will not be disclosed. Some of the better systems even provide color graphics in their chart presentations and allow the trader the option of printing out the calculations, the worksheet, and the charts. Being able to get the charts onto hard copy is a significant advantage; it permits further study of the analysis and enables the trader to superimpose any of his other lines or studies on the same chart.

The next logical questions to address are: What does a trading system consist of, how do you operate it, and what is the end product of the system? Excluding those few basic numerical systems that don't use a calculator or a computer, a trading system consists of two parts—hardware and software. For hardware, you use either a programmable calculator (such as a powerful Hewlett Packard) or one of the microcomputers. You need some method of inputting daily price data, and that can either be done manually or by connecting into a remote data bank such as Commodity Systems Inc.'s QUICKTRIEVE®[4] To complete this connection you need a phone modem (and a plug-in wall module). Normally, you need two disk drives (or a hard-disk model) and a minimum of 256K memory. In terms of software, if you are using a programmable calculator, you need some way to "instruct" the calculator as to the computations, and this can be done in the form of small modules that fit into an access slot in the calculator. Most of the systems, however, run on a micro, and you generally use two disks, a program disk (that instructs the micro as to procedure) and a data disk. The data disk is updated daily, either through manual input or connection with a data bank via phone modem. Data update consists of either actual prices or perpetual prices. Perpetuals are a continuous series of prices that are calculated by

---

[4]Commodity Systems Inc., 200 W. Palmetto Pk. Road, Boca Raton, FL 33432

the data bank (the 91-day perpetual is a popular form) and that tend to smooth some of the gaps and imbalances in actual price data. There are many advantages to using perpetual data. One is that it eliminates the need to reenter and recalculate your price data every time a futures month expires. Perpetual data is just that—perpetual and continuous.

The procedure starts by inputting the day's prices; updating occurs each evening following the day's close. If you don't do it manually, you will have a separate software program for this; the process takes a few minutes at most. Once the price data has been input into your computer, and then transferred from your computer onto your data disk, you remove the data acquisition disk from your computer and boot up your program disk. Depending on the speed of your hardware and complexity of your program, running the program can take anywhere from 15 to 40 minutes. During this interval, the computer is calculating the stops and other signals based on the formulas on the program disk and the prices on the data disk. Then a near-magical thing happens— your printer comes to life and out of it emerges a printout containing the various prices and signals.

Some years ago, I was demonstrating a computer system to a colleague, and my young son, then aged 8, quietly observed the discussion. He was interested in the proceedings because he occasionally ran the system for me. At a lull in the conversation, apparently unable to restrain himself further, Charlie blurted out to my guest, "And he cheats—he gets the right answers out of the printer." Well, I wouldn't exactly describe what emerges from the printer as "the right answers," although we always hope they will be. Printouts come in all sizes and formats, but typically look something like Figure 12−1. This particular system runs on either an Apple, an IBM, or one of the compatibles, and follows 16 markets. Each evening, it provides a printout containing the recommended position long or short, plus how many units (from one to three, depending on the strength of the trend). It then provides the market close for the day under review (in Figure 12−1, all prices are basis 91-day perpetual), the point for the reversal stop, and three other columns dealing with putting on or liquidating pyramid positions. Operators who play just a single contract or who are not concerned with pyramiding are not necessarily concerned with the final three columns in this particular system.

FIGURE 12−1 Daily Printout from a Long-Term Trading System Introduced in May 1983
This particular system runs on either an Apple, IBM, or one of the compatibles, and utilizes perpetual data in its calculations.

K/W LONG TERM TRADING SYSTEM DAILY WORK SHEET   03 / 13 / 87

	Position Long	Short	1 Close	2 Stop	3 1st Pyr.	4 2nd Pyramid	5
CORN		3	1598	* 1680	1568	1631	1500
WHEAT		2	2744	* 2841	2770	2821	2643
SOYBEANS		3	4923	* 5063	4885	5001	4801
COTTON #2		3	5616	* 5802	5493	5682	5199
SUGAR #11	3		820	* 781	816	851	749
LIVE HOGS	3		4711	4385	4582	4661	4386
COFFEE		3	10487	13077	11329	13031	10668
NY L CRUDE	2		1778	* 1718	1750	1831	1629
H.OIL #2		3	4800	* 4923	4686	4975	4341
COMEX GOLD	2		4082	* 3959	4095	4167	3964
NY SILVER	3		565	* 534	560	570	546
JAPAN YEN	3		6606	6428	6553	6638	6507
SWISS FR		3	6477	* 6516	6483	6727	6404
T. BILLS		2	9449	* 9464	9447	9469	9421
S&P STOCK	3		29104	25874	28869	29274	27478
SOY.OIL		2	1613	* 1546	1612	1712	1564

As you can readily see, a system is quite specific and exact, although there are a few systems whose analysis is subjective and dependent on the operator's interpretation. Another significant feature of a good system is that it suffers no bias for the long side of every market, as do the majority of traders. All signals are derived from the mathematics within the program analyzing the prices of the last X days (anything from 6 to 72 days, depending on the particular system).

In the final analysis, it boils down to this: A trading system is a tool, and, like most tools, there are quality ones and mediocre ones. A system certainly isn't the ultimate answer to consistent profits in the markets, and there are plenty of successful operators who wouldn't know the difference between a data disk and a slipped disk. However, the right system can be a significant aid in your overall trading. But—and here comes the big "but"—its benefit will be proportional to the patience and discipline with which you approach and use it.

Trending/Anti-Trending—A Dual Market Approach

The ideal formula for investment success is the appropriate integration of a good technical system with sound principles of strategy and money management. But creating and then implementing this balance is easier said than done. During the 30 odd years that I've been trading, I've made my share of killings and had perhaps more than my share of getting killed. In my experience, the most profitable and consistent approach is a long-term positioning strategy—getting aboard in the early stage of a major move, pyramiding at the propitious time, and staying aboard for the ride. However, there is a fundamental pitfall in the way most operators handle this strategy.

Regrettably, we are always trying to project a distinct (up or down) price trend out of every market situation. As a result, we are invariably buying on strength at what we perceive to be the bullish moment and then haphazardly selling on weakness whenever it appears to be a bearish moment. Red ink abounds on most of these trades. "How come I'm always buying on rallies and then selling on the reactions?" Does that sound familiar?

The simple truth is that markets are in relative equilibrium most of the time; that is, in a broad, random sideways range rather than a distinct up or down trending mode. A graphic example of this buy high, sell low tactic was the crude oil market for the three years from 1983 through 1985, when the market traded broadly between 26.00 and 32.00 (see Figure 13–1). Every rally toward 30.00–32.00 was accompanied by computer and other technical upflips, while each subsequent reaction back towards 26.00–28.00 would predictably flip everyone down.

As a viable alternative to this "oops" method of trading and after years of probing and testing, making more mistakes than I care to recall, I have developed a dual trading approach to specu-

---

FIGURE 13–1 Long-Term Weekly (Nearest Future) Crude Oil
For the three-year period, 1983–85, crude oil traded in a broad sideways range bounded by 26.00 to 32.00. Long-term position traders were whipsawed as their systems kept giving buy signals on the rallies towards the upper boundary of the range and sell signals on reactions toward the lower boundary. Their patience was finally rewarded, however, in January of 1986, when the market broke down through the bottom of the trading range and continued south till it reached the 11.00 level. This points out the need for consistent adherence to *all* trading signals because the one big profit on the early January down-leg exceeded the string of small losses during the sideways trading range.

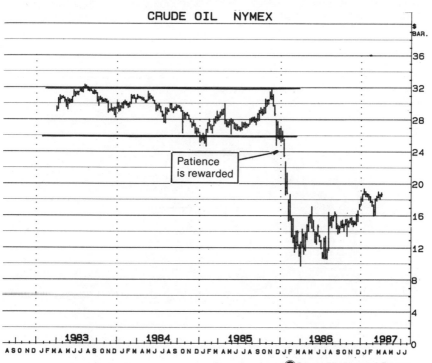

CRUDE OIL   NYMEX

Patience is rewarded

Commodity Research Bureau

lation. It can be summarized as follows: During periods of broad, sideways price movement, you play an essentially antitrending game—buying on reactions towards the lower boundary of the trading range and selling on rallies towards the upper boundary. However, once the market blasts out of this broad sideways formation—in either direction—you abandon the antitrending position and follow the breakout strength (see Figures 13–2 and 13–3).

FIGURE 13–2   June 1987 T Bills

The market was locked within a broad sideways trading range (94.45 to 95.00) for the six-month period, August 1986 through January 1987. During this sideways period, you would play antitrend, looking to place shorts against the 95.00 upper boundary and to cover shorts and go long against the 94.45 lower boundary. These antitrend positions would be protected with stops *on close only*, just beyond the trading range (at 94.35 stop close and 95.10 stop close). On a closing breakout in either direction, you would liquidate your antitrending position and assume a new trending position. On February 10, the market broke down, with June closing at 94.31. On the close, the position would have been reversed from long to short.

Reverse from long to short

Ⓒ **Commodity Research Bureau**

FIGURE 13-3   Long-Term Weekly (Nearest Future) Coffee
The market traded within a sideways range (130.00 to 160.00) for 27 months, from July 1983 through October 1985. You should have played this antitrend, going short against the 160.00 upper boundary and reversing to long against the 130.00 lower boundary. These antitrend positions would have been protected with *on close only* stops, just beyond the trading range, around 127.00 and 163.00. Following several successful antitrend trades, the market broke out on the upside in October 1985. The short position would have been liquidated, and a with-the-trend long position would have been taken.

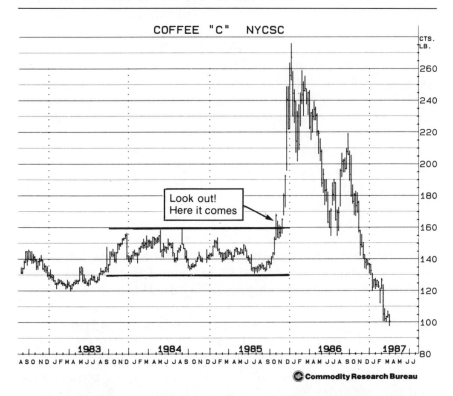

COFFEE "C" NYCSC

© Commodity Research Bureau

This approach is logical and straightforward, with no fancy "bells and whistles," as in so many of the current systems and trading theories. Here is an optimum market approach, coordinated into two aspects—the technical trading system *and* the investment strategy. When followed in a serious and disciplined manner, by either a speculator, trade hedger, or financial institution, it could yield consistent market profits within an acceptable risk environment. It constitutes the game plan for many successful professional operators, who may keep their winning strategies to themselves but whose profitable results are highly acclaimed.

To implement the strategy, you start by identifying the price trend of each market as sideways or trending (up or down).

How do you identify the trend as being sideways or trending? I usually do it by inspection, studying both the daily and the weekly charts for each commodity under review. A discussion regarding trend identification is not within the scope of this book, but there are good reference sources available. A more objective method of trend identification is through the use of some available formula, and the best I have seen is Wilder's *Directional Movement Index*. This index measures, on a scale between 0 and 100, the extent to which any market is trending. Values in the upper end of the scale indicate a strong trending market, while lower values accompany nontrending (sideways) markets. The index also defines and identifies an equilibrium point, where directional movement up is just equal to directional movement down. You can calculate these values by hand, but it is more efficient to use either a programmable calculator, such as one of the Hewlett Packards, or a microcomputer (Apple, IBM, or a compatible). Information concerning software packages is available from Trend Research, Ltd.[1]

The other approach to trend identification is via a subscription to one of the commercial services which provides this information on a daily or weekly basis. For several years, I have used the Computer Trend Analyzer, contained in the weekly CRB Futures Chart Service (see Figure 13–4). This technical method is based on mathematical calculations of price movements, which include moving averages, volatility, oscillators, and time cycles. The weekly service is actually an offshoot of CRB's daily Electronic Trend Analyzer, which includes trend identification plus other technical information for some 200 futures contracts. As you can see from Figure 13–4, the Computer Trend Analyzer identifies the trend of each market as sideways, up or down. For each sideways market, it identifies the support and resistance levels. A close below the indicated support price will flip the trend to down, and a close above the indicated resistance price will flip

---

[1]J. Welles Wilder, Jr., *New Concepts in Technical Trading Systems* (Mcleansville, N.C. 27301: Trend Research, 1978).

FIGURE 13-4

COMPUTER TREND ANALYZER

Commodity	Delivery	Computer Trend	Trend Started Date	Trend Started Price	Current Computer Support	Current Computer Resistance	Market Close 2/6/87	Week's Change
CRB FUTURES	MAR. '87	UP	1/14/87	214.10	212.50		213.45	- .35%
BRITISH POUND #	MAR. '87	SIDE FROM UP	2/6/86	1.4995	1.5238		1.4995	- $.0055
CATTLE (Live)	APRIL '87	UP	1/12/87	58.40	59.90		62.67	- .20¢
COCOA	MAR. '87	SIDEWAYS	1/23/87	1815	1769	1937	1839	+ $19
COFFEE "C"	MAR. '87	DOWN	10/10/86	177.83		131.15	126.54	+ 2.56¢
COPPER	MAR. '87	DOWN	1/20/87	60.20		61.65	60.90	+ .50¢
CORN	MAR. '87	DOWN	11/24/86	175 1/2		161 1/2	154 3/4	- 2 1/4¢
COTTON #2	MAR. '87	DOWN	1/28/87	55.15		59.65	54.77	- .41¢
CRUDE OIL	APRIL '87	UP	12/11/86	15.68	18.05		18.40	- .18¢
DEUTSCHE MARK #	MAR. '87	SIDE FROM UP	2/6/86	.5026	.5300	.5581	.5390	- $.0078
EURODOLLAR	MAR. '87	DOWN	1/26/87	93.89		93.98	93.67	- .02%
GAS (Unleaded)	APRIL '87	UP	12/12/86	45.40	51.20		52.59	+ .01¢
GOLD (Comex)	APRIL '87	UP	1/7/87	408.00	403.50		407.40	- $1.5
HEATING OIL#2 #	APRIL '87	SIDE FROM UP	2/4/87	48.85	48.05	51.30	49.98	- 1.06¢
HOGS	APRIL '87	UP	1/30/87	45.97	43.65		45.27	- .70¢
JAPANESE YEN	MAR. '87	UP	12/26/86	.6301	.6450		.6488	- $.0028
LUMBER	MAR. '87	UP	1/12/87	173.00	180.00		202.30	+ $14.40
MMI - MAXI	MAR. '87	UP	1/5/87	380.25	403.70		422.60	+ 6.35pts
MUNI - BONDS	MAR. '87	UP	12/23/86	100-03	100-11		101-18	+ 25/32
NYSE (NYFE)	MAR. '87	UP	1/6/87	145.40	152.20		160.55	+ 4.30pts
ORANGE JUICE	MAR. '87	DOWN	12/31/86	124.00		126.78	122.50	+ 2.30¢
PLATINUM	APRIL '87	UP	1/9/87	523.80	505.00		525.60	- $2.10
PORK BELLIES	MAY '87	DOWN	12/31/86	65.77		66-90	65.27	+ .82¢
SILVER (N.Y.)	MAR. '87	UP	1/14/87	564.00	548.30		556.00	+ 3.50¢
SOYBEANS	MAR. '87	SIDEWAYS	1/19/87	499 1/4	489 1/2	504 1/2	492 1/4	- 8¢
SOYBEAN MEAL ##	MAR. '87	UP FROM DOWN	2/3/87	146.30	141.90		145.50	+ $1.30
SOYBEAN OIL	MAR. '87	UP	1/16/87	16.15	15.95		16.21	- .5¢
S&P 500	MAR. '87	UP	1/6/87	253.55	266.60		281.20	+ 7.05pts
SUGAR "11"	MAR. '87	UP	1/13/87	6.74	6.95		7.43	- .31¢
SWISS FRANC	MAR. '87	UP	12/23/87	.6123	.6400		.6406	- $.0088
T-BILLS (IMM)	MAR. '87	DOWN	1/27/87	94.63		94.75	94.40	- .10¢%
T-BONDS (CBoT)	MAR. '87	SIDEWAYS	1/26/87	99-15	99-07	100-31	100-17	+ 27/32
T-NOTES (CBoT) #	MAR. '87	SIDE FROM UP	2/2/87	104	103-24	104-24	104-15	+ 9/32
VALUE LINE (K.C.)	MAR. '87	UP	1/6/87	236.55	243.30		257.95	+ 12.10 pts
WHEAT (Chi)	MAR. '87	UP	1/14/87	283	281		288	- 1/4¢

#TREND CHANGES ##TREND REVERSALS *CONTRACT TRANSFERS

(C) **Commodity Research Bureau**

the trend to up. Furthermore, in the case of up- or down-trending markets, the Analyzer indicates where an up market flips to side (price closes below the indicated support price) and where a down market flips to side (price closes above the indicated resistance price).

For each sideways market, you identify the following:

1. The upper and lower boundaries of the SIDEWAYS formation.
2. The price levels ("exit trade") where, *on a closing basis,* the trend will have changed from sideways to up (upside breakout) or from sideways to down (downside breakout).

These exit trade (stop) points where you close out your anti-trend position *and* put on a trending position will be beyond the boundaries of the sideways trading range. The buy stop, to exit your short antitrend position, will be above the upper boundary of the trading range. The sell stop, to exit your long antitrend position, will be below the lower boundary. How much above and below? That is, obviously, the trickiest part of the operation because, if the stop is too close you will be excessively whipsawed; if the stop is too far, you will be taking some whopping losses. You should consider the total loss you are willing to take on the position. Then set your stop at the point beyond your trade entry point that would limit the loss to this sum. For an example, if you are trading soybeans and have set a risk limit of, say, $600 (12 cents), you would set your sell stop (for a long position) 12 cents below your buy price and your buy stop (for a short position) 12 cents above your sell price. Take the case of March 1987 soybeans (Figure 13–5). They are trading in a broad sideways range between 4.80 and 5.10, with the current market at 4.89. You would be interested in buying around 4.86 with a sell stop at 4.74 (12 cent risk). Or you could go short around 5.04 with a buy stop at 5.16 (again, 12 cent risk).

In terms of liquidating the position, I would take the trade one stop further by setting my protective stops as stop *and* reverse. If the market were to close at my buy or sell stop, each of which is 6 cents beyond the limit of the trading range, I would want to reverse to the respective trending position. If I had sold 10M short at 5.04, I would buy 20M at 5.16 *stop on close.* If I had bought 10M at 4.86, I would sell 20M at 4.74 *stop on close.*

FIGURE 13–5 March 1987 Soybeans

The market is trading within a broad range bounded by 4.80 and 5.10. So long as it remains within this range, we play antitrend. We buy on reactions to 4.86 and sell on rallies to 5.04. On a close above 5.16 the trend will reverse from side to up, and we cover shorts and reverse to long. On a close below 4.74 the trend will reverse from side to down, and we liquidate longs and reverse to short.

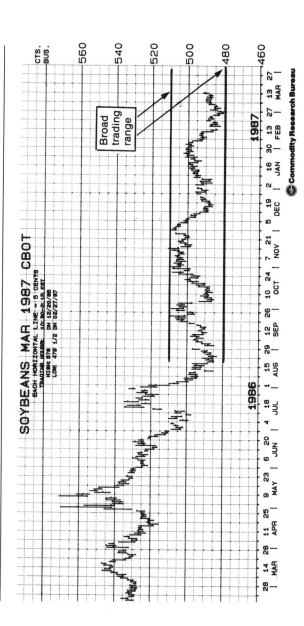

SOYBEANS MAR 1987 CBOT
EACH HORIZONTAL LINE = 5 CENTS
TRADING HOURS: 10:30-2:15 EST
HIGH 578   DN 12/20/85
LOW 479 1/2 DN 02/27/87

Broad trading range

1986

1987

However, if the position goes your way, since you are trading antitrend, you will liquidate and reverse at the opposite side of the trading range. If you had sold 10M March beans on strength at 5.04 and the market started heading south, you would buy 20M at 4.86. Conversely, if your first trade was a buy against the lower boundary at 4.86 and the market rallied, you would sell 20M at 5.04.

The strategic aspects of this operation dictate that, while trading antitrend, your stops are stop *and* reverse. Also, they are *on close only*. You do not want to be stopped and reversed by some random intraday jump outside the trading range, only to find that by the close the price may have returned back within the range.

In terms of how to exit a trending position, you will do this through being stopped out—whether at a profit or a loss. Your initial stop on a trending position should be placed to limit your loss to an acceptable amount, perhaps to 80 to 100 percent of the margin requirements (or less, if that is excessive). If the market does move favorably, you are still faced with the problem of exiting this (profitable) position. Experience has shown that there is no viable and consistent way for you to pick off major tops and bottoms. All of us have had the frustrating experience of dumping a favorable with-the-trend position prematurely. Therefore, it makes good sense to sit with the position until the *market* takes you out. You do this by setting efficient stops, advancing them as the market moves favorably, until you are ultimately stopped out.

Being stopped out of a trending position (here, you stop out intraday rather than on close) does not necessarily mean that the trend has reversed. It may just mean that you reached your pain threshhold and you deemed it prudent to cut losses or to preserve part of your profit. Use a straight liquidating stop, not a reversal stop. Assuming that the major trend had not changed, you can always reenter the market at a more propitious time.

Although the dual trend/antitrend strategy is logical, it may be emotionally difficult to stick with. Considering the volatility of many markets, it really takes a strong constitution to play this successfully. We ought to examine why there is such a compelling temptation on the part of many speculators to buy near the top of a broad sideways trading range and to sell near the bottom. It is largely a matter of "crowd perception," for markets invariably seem most bullish on the rallies and most bearish on the reactions. As a market surges towards the top of a broad sideways range, there will be lots of bullish news and rumors and higher price expectations, accompanied by broad speculative buying. After all, no one wants to miss the start of the big "bull express." This would probably turn out alright if we were talking about buying into a bullish trending market or selling into a bearish trending market. But, since most markets move in a sideways random direction most of the time, this "buy high and sell low" approach is invariably the wrong way to play. In fact, much of the speculative buying on strength and selling on weakness during sideways nontrends is played to advantage by professional operators who unload their positions held from better levels.

I recently talked to a Washington-based international banker, who had spent the morning with a senior bond trader at one of the large money-center banks. "Imagine," he gasped, "the guy buys $100 million bonds in the morning and then dumps the position before lunch. The loss was $100,000 and nobody batted an eye."

Clearly the banks, commercial dealers, big institutions, and floor operators play a dynamic and broad-swinging game—big orders, big positions, for big dollars. The result is big profits and losses, but even bigger swings and volatility. And, since their orientation is essentially short-term, we longer-term position traders find it increasingly difficult to stick with our prescribed holding strategies. We are, all too often, mauled in the crossfire between the big professional or commercial houses and the heavy concentration of commission firm and commodity fund stop orders that are frequently used as "target practice" by professional operators.

There isn't much you can do to prevent these massive whipsaw moves. But you can minimize the damage by taking smaller positions and trading less frequently. Also, try to avoid buying strength and selling weakness in broad sideways trends, since these are the typical speculator traps set up by the major players.

The dual trend/antitrend strategy, if used correctly and in an objective and disciplined manner, should considerably improve your overall trading results.

CHAPTER FOURTEEN

Taking Advantage of Recurring Seasonal Tendencies

Although it was William Shakespeare who said, "Beware the Ides of March," it was S. Kroll who said, "I'm not so concerned about March (besides, it's my birthday). It's February that's giving me fits!"

As we arrive at the month of March each year, I breathe a sigh of relief. That's because January and February are consistently the most vexing months for the trend-following commodity trader. Market action is extra volatile, and price fluctuations seemingly random.

February, in particular, coincides with what I call the *February break*. This is the period when even well-entrenched bull markets take a reactionary respite and ongoing bear trends seem to accelerate their decline. The February break had its roots in the grain trade, where producers would tend to hold each year's crops off the market till the beginning of the following year. This strategy gave them two benefits: They deferred their tax liability on the crop, and their first-quarter sales provided money for April 15 tax payments plus funds for general farm purposes. And although agricultural markets constitute a much smaller percentage of futures trading today than in former years, this entrenched tradition of the February break still exists. And it continues to be a significant market factor.

Is there a way that the technical trader can take advantage of this phenomenon? You bet there is! First of all, be a bit wary of new long positions, especially in the agriculturals, during this period. If I got a buy signal, I would take the trade but not with the same degree of confidence (take a smaller position than usual) as for a short position on a sell signal.

However, there is another intriguing aspect of this February break that can significantly benefit both the hedger and the long-term trader. Starting in early March, keep a close watch on your daily charts and draw a red horizontal line at the level of the January-February closing high. This provides you with a particularly efficient buy stop to either take on a new long position or to cover shorts and flip to long. This level is likely to be a formidable resistance point, which should be difficult for many markets to overcome (see Figures 14-1 and 14-2). The rationale to buy on stop above this level is that you want to be long whichever markets have sufficient strength to surpass, *on a closing basis*, their January/February high close. Further, a strong weekly close would be even more significant than a daily close. Not all markets will be able to surpass this level, and these should probably be played short, or not at all. Notwithstanding this rather simplistic trading strategy, all positions should still be protected with reasonable stops at your personal pain threshold, whether it's a specific dollar figure or a percentage of the margin requirement.

The February break is just one of the seasonal price tendencies that affects futures prices on a recurring basis. However, each futures market has seasonal characteristics particular to its own set of supply and demand factors. If you understand these, you'll be a better trader.

It was W. D. Gann, one of the giants of futures speculation, who first underscored the importance of seasonality in futures analysis. His classic work, *How to Make Profits Trading Commodities*,[1] devotes considerable attention to the concept of seasonality as a powerful tool in price analysis. As an example, Gann identified the seasonal trends for wheat for the period from 1841

---

[1] *How to Make Profits Trading Commodities* (Lambert-Gann Publishing Co., Inc., 1942, revised 1951).

FIGURE 14−1   July 1987 Sugar

Sugar's strong uptrend stalled at the level of its January/February highs. A line across these highs, at 8.60, provides an efficient buy stop, on a closing basis, to either go long, or to add to previously held long positions. Short players can sell against this level, using the closing penetration of 8.60 as a reversal stop.

to 1941. According to his analysis, the market reached extreme low prices the following number of times during each calendar month of the year, over the 101-year period.

January	2 times	July	6 times
February	7 times	August	16 times
March	12 times	September	8 times
April	14 times	October	13 times
May	5 times	November	10 times
June	9 times	December	12 times

FIGURE 14–2 July 1987 Corn

A classic bear market. The reaction was clearly accelerated during the January/February period. A line drawn across the January/February highs at 1.72 defines a significant zone of major resistance. You can add additional shorts against this resistance level, say around 1.66. The 1.72 top provides an efficient buy stop, on a closing basis, to cover shorts and flip to long.

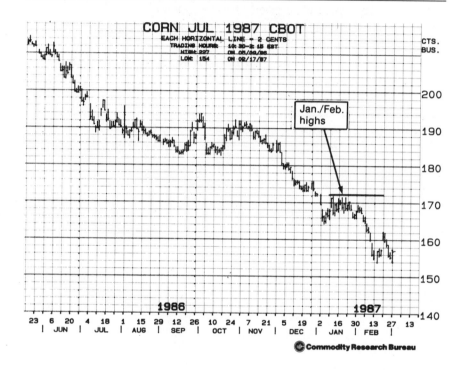

Gann's analysis noted that the month of August, just following the harvest, scored the most lows. He recommended that, when the market reaches lows in March or April, you buy for the rally because most tops come out in May. Then, if you do get the strength in May or early June, you should sell short, anticipating the seasonal trend to result in low levels in August.

Another acclaimed trader who did considerable research into seasonal tendencies was Ralph Ainsworth.[2] He published the Ainsworth Financial Service, one of the leading grain forecasting

---

[2]Ralph M. Ainsworth, *Profitable Grain Trading* (Greenville, S.C.: Traders Press, 1933, reprinted 1980).

services of the 1930s. It was said that his basic timing system consisted of a number of proprietary Grain Trading Calendars (this one for wheat).

Feb 22   BUY WHEAT, following the bearish effect of the first Argentine crop run.

Jul 1   BUY WHEAT, on likely price deterioration following a period of good crop prospects.

Nov 28   BUY WHEAT, before the news of crop damage from the Southern Hemisphere.

Jan 10   SELL WHEAT, because it is apt to have advanced too high and may be overbought.

FIGURE 14–3 Weekly Seasonal Chart of July Soybeans
There seems to be a strong seasonal uptrend from mid-February (coinciding with the February break) through the expiration of the July future. The contract tends to expire near the highs. Lows made late in the previous year are tested in January, and upside penetration of the January high often triggers the seasonal move.

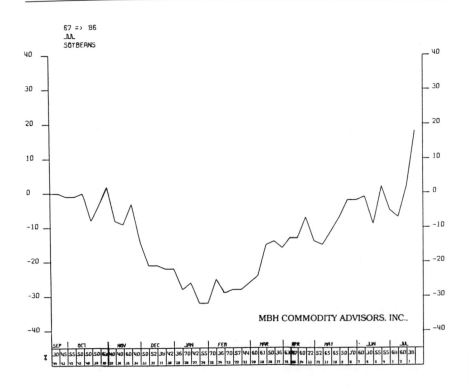

May 10   SELL WHEAT, as this should be the last of the
          winter kill scare.
Sep 10   SELL WHEAT, as this could follow the black rust
          scare.

After reviewing these seasonal trading systems, one has the
distinct feeling that we've come a long way since the empirical
and subjective studies of the 1930s and 40s. However, it wasn't
until the availability of powerful computers and software that
analysts were able to exploit, and go far beyond, the studies of
Gann, Ainsworth, and others.

The leading proponent of seasonal studies is Jake Bernstein,
who has combined modern computer technology with an objective
research approach. His, *MBH Seasonal Futures Charts,*[3] published annually, presents a computer study of weekly seasonal
futures tendencies. This soft-cover volume focuses on some 25
futures from all the actively traded markets. Besides containing
an excellent collection of seasonal charts, it also offers the most
informative discussion of seasonal price analysis that I've ever
seen. Bernstein first offered a seasonal chart study (1953–1977)
of cash commodities in 1977, followed two years later by his
Seasonal Chart Study of Commodity Spreads. Over the years, he
has improved and expanded these guides with the assistance of
powerful computer equipment (see Figures 14–3 and 14–4).

The current version presents, in both chart and tabular form,
the recurring seasonal tendencies for a broad range of futures,
including the percentage of years when the price of each future,
for each week in the year, was up or down. In his foreword to the
collection, publisher Bernstein notes that there are regrettably
too few traders who really understand how to derive maximum
benefit from seasonal studies. Too frequently, the speculator will
refer to a particular seasonal merely to help justify an existing
market position, and if the study does not agree with his position,
he will somehow rationalize the disparity and end up ignoring the
seasonal.

From a strategic point of view, seasonal considerations stack
up as an important device in the technical trader's toolkit. It is

---

[3]*MBH Seasonal Futures Charts* (Winnetka, Ill.: MBH Commodity Advisors, published annually).

FIGURE 14-4 Weekly Seasonal Chart of December Cotton
The December future seems to show the best seasonality of all cotton futures.
From a seasonal low around April, the contract tends towards seasonal
strength. Note that the up and down swings in cotton can be quite violent.

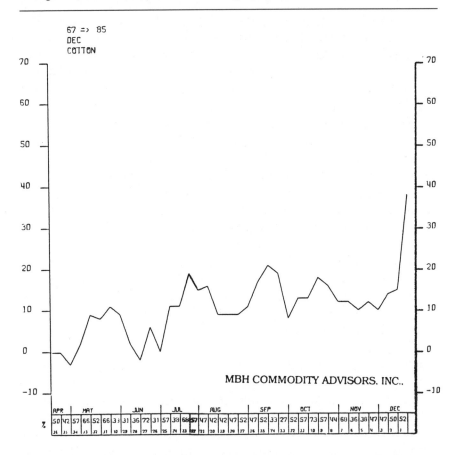

not a standalone technique, nor can it be used as a substitute for a
good system or other technical approach. But it can be used to
confirm or reject, trading conclusions based on other techniques. I
would not do long-term position trading without checking out the
relevant seasonal studies, than I would fish for bluefish without
consulting the fishing calendar. February is a poor month for
bluefish!

Keep What Shows the Best Profit: Close Out the Biggest Loss

The late 1980s have witnessed some of the toughest and most frustrating futures markets in recent memory. Good trading strategy mandates that you should be able to profit with equal facility in both up and down markets. But, during many campaigns, we have experienced markets that have appeared to be moving both up *and* down nearly simultaneously. Many solid uptrends have been punctuated with violent downside reactions. These price slides briefly abort the uptrend by stopping out speculative long positions. And, after the stops have been "cleaned out," the market resumes its northerly course. Meanwhile, quite a few bear markets have experienced equally violent rallies. The rally cleans out the speculative protective buy stops, knocking the so-called weak holders out of their profitable short positions. Then the bear market resumes.

The hot breath of the margin clerk is being felt more frequently than ever before due to the erratic and violent nature of countertrend swings. What should you do when confronted with the familiar windowed envelope that you know is the call for margin? Over the years, I have had countless conversations and correspondence with traders concerning the strategy of dealing with margin calls. In general, they are ambivalent and inconsistent in their response to calls, and seek guidance in terms of a viable, strategic approach.

There are two types of calls—*new business* and *maintenance.* Of the two, maintenance calls are far more common. Exchange regulations require that new business calls be met with new funds, not with liquidation. However, maintenance calls may be met either with deposit of new funds or by reducing positions.

Most traders make the wrong decision when confronted with the inevitable margin call. The options are: Put up new money or reduce positions and, if reducing positions, which one(s) to close out to meet the call. In most circumstances, I do not recommend putting up new funds to meet a maintenance call. The call is a clear signal that the account is underperforming, or at least that some of the positions are underperforming, and there is no logic in trying to defend bad positions with new money. The appropriate tactic is to liquidate some positions to eliminate the margin call and reduce your risk exposure. But, if you close positions to reduce risk, aren't you also reducing your profit potential and your ability to regain a profitable footing? Reducing positions yet maintaining your profit potential sounds like a hypothetical goal, but how can you actually achieve it? You do it with a basic strategy that is known to successful floor traders but unfortunately not to commission house speculators to any degree. You close out those positions that show the biggest paper losses when marked to the market, especially if they are antitrending. This clearly reduces your loss exposure by eliminating the positions that are carrying the biggest losses. Yet by holding on to your most successful positions, which are obviously being held on the right side of the trending markets, you have maintained your potential to profit. The odds clearly favor ultimate profits on profitable with-the-trend positions over losing antitrend positions.

Regrettably, most speculators choose to close out the profitable positions while holding onto the losing ones. "After all," they reason, "no one ever goes broke taking a profit." But no one ever gets rich taking small profits, especially in trending markets with big potential. The strategy of closing profitable positions and holding onto losing ones is costly, frequently ruinous, and typical of unsuccessful traders. Conversely, one of the hallmarks of successful operators is their ability, coupled with the discipline, to close out losing positions and stick with the winning ones. And, while it may be more ego-satisfying to take profits rather than losses, we are not playing for ego here. We are playing for big plus figures at the bottom line with reasonable risks. In that context, you should be more concerned with an overall profitable operation than in proving yourself right and the market wrong.

There is a corollary here that professional floor operators use as a proven strategy. In any given market or in two related markets, you buy the strongest-acting future and sell the weakest-acting. This tends to hedge your bet because, if the market advances, your long leg should outperform your short leg; if the market declines, your short leg should be weaker than the long. And, as an accompanying bonus, you frequently get a reduced margin on the position, or, for the same dollar margin, you can put on a bigger position. As an example, the Chicago corn market has been in a major downtrend from late 1983 to at least early 1987. The wheat market, on the other hand, has been trending generally higher, providing technical or systems traders a succession of quite reliable buy signals. Suppose you got a sell signal in corn and put on a short position in, say, June of 1986. Your margin on each 5,000-bushel contract would probably have been $400. Then let's suppose that you got a good buy signal in wheat in October of the same year and put on some longs. Your margin on each wheat contract would normally be $750. So for each wheat (long) and corn (short) contract, you might expect to have to post $1,150 in margin. Have we got a deal for you! You don't have to put up $1,150 for the wheat/corn position. You don't even have to put up $750 (the higher of the two legs). In fact, you can put on the position for a measly margin of $500. I don't approve of trading on such thin margin and would prefer to post the required margin on the greater of the two sides ($750 in this case). But that's still tremendous leverage, and it doesn't take very much of a math whiz to calculate the profit, either in dollar terms or as a percentage of margin, that was made during this period in the wheat/corn (spread) position (you do it on your calculator—mine only goes out to seven figures). A tough analysis? Perhaps—but not too tough if you had opted to buy the stronger market (the wheat) and sold the weaker (the corn). See Figure 15−1. An alternative means of timing these spread (also called straddle or switch) trades is by using spread charts, such as those published weekly in the CRB Futures Chart Service by Commodity Research Bureau (see Figure 15−2). Here you put on and take off the position as a spread, and you time your trades on the basis of price differences. For example, in the wheat versus corn position shown in the accompanying chart (15−2), the market went from wheat 63 cents over corn to 1.05 over. Assuming you caught just half the 42 cent move, you would have scored a profit of 21 cents, equal to $1,000 (after commission) and over 100 percent profit on your margin.

FIGURE 15−1   July 1987 Wheat and July 1987 Corn
You buy the strength (wheat) and sell the weakness (corn). This is the type of situation that many professional operators seek; it has good profit potential, reasonable risk, and low margin. Opportunities like this appear every year—and the trader should be alert to the chance to buy the strength and sell the weakness. For entry timing, you can take signals from whichever technical or trading system you have confidence in and time each leg on the basis of these signals.

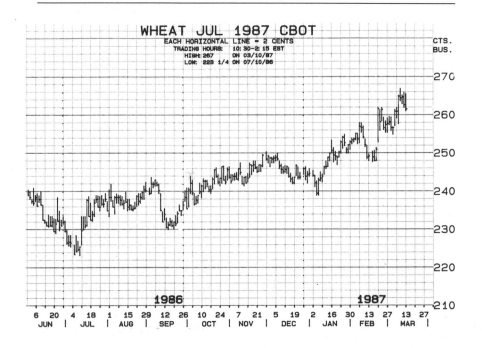

Yet another aspect of this *buy strength, sell weakness* strategy can provide extra profits to knowledgeable operators. An important feature of many big bull markets is a price inversion, also called an inverted market, in which nearby futures gain in price relative to distant ones and ultimately sell at premiums to the nearbys. This is due to a tightness—or a perceived tightness—in spot (nearby) supplies. Traders should watch these switch differentials carefully, because an inversion, or even a significant tightening of the normal premiums between futures months, could provide an important confirmation of a developing bull situation. In fact, I generally add another 25 to 50 percent to any long position I may be carrying following such a price inversion, *on a closing basis.*

In addition, professional operators are always on the alert for developing price inversions, and at the first sign of an inversion (on a closing basis), there are spread traders who buy the pre-

---

FIGURE 15−1 *(Concluded)*

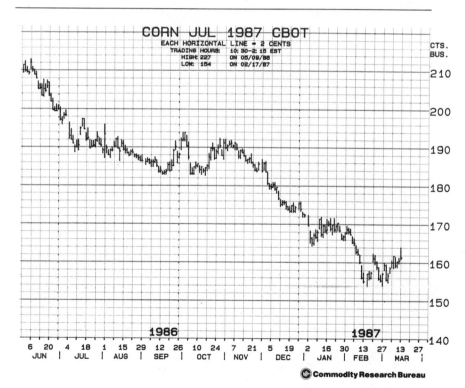

FIGURE 15–2   July 1987 Wheat versus Corn Spread Chart
As an alternative method of timing spread (buy strength versus sell weakness)
trades, you can use spread charts. These charts are available for a broad
selection of related markets or two different futures in the same market. You
can enter and liquidate positions on the basis of price differences. As an
example, let's assume you put on long wheat versus short corn at wheat 70
cents over corn, and the current difference has widened to 1.00 over (you have
a 30 cent profit on the position). If you want to stop out if the difference
narrowed to, say 90 cents, you would enter the following order. "Buy (quantity)
corn and sell (quantity) wheat at 90 cents stop, premium on the wheat." With
this order, you would be locking in your profit at 20 cents, less breakage
and commissions.

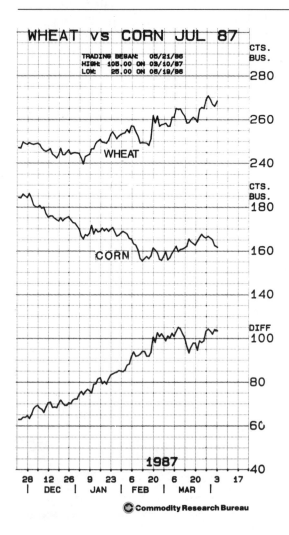

WHEAT vs CORN JUL 87

TRADING BEGAN: 05/21/86
HIGH: 105.00 ON 03/10/87
LOW: 25.00 ON 06/19/86

Commodity Research Bureau

mium future and sell the discount. Granted, you have to be pretty nimble to play this game because the inversion could unwind at any time. But while it lasts, you can score some good profits with reasonable risks. In summary, it doesn't matter how you label this strategy—keep the profitable positions and close out the losers, buy the strength and sell the weakness, or go long the premium and short the discount. What is important is that you are aware of it, you identify your strong-weak markets accurately, and you apply this strategy in a consistent and disciplined manner.

PART FOUR

On Conducting a Trading Campaign

The Man They Called J. L.

As the plump aluminum bird curved westward toward Fort Lauderdale, the luminescent color delineation between the Gulf Stream and the ocean was outstanding. I slumped back in my seat while the jumbo began its final approach, reflecting on the main reason for my Florida fishing trip this Christmas vacation. I felt a compelling fellowship for a man they called J. L., and I was here because he used to come here.

I could picture him in his heyday in the 1920s, tall, trim, and intense, seated by the window of the speeding New York – Florida express. Anticipating days of fishing and fellowship, relaxation and contemplation—and most important a respite, albeit brief, from his heroic battles in the arenas of Wall Street and Chicago. His name was Jesse Lauriston Livermore.

Throughout this century, scores of brilliant or lucky market operators have had the heady and envious sensation of closing a position with a seven-figure (to the left of the decimal point) profit. I myself, on a few rare occasions, have been fortunate enough to have been included in this exclusive group. But Livermore was in a class by himself. For the sheer scope and magnitude of his gutsy operations, for the disciplined and calculating way in which he bought and sold, for the lonely and detached hand that he invariably played, he has never been surpassed by any operator.

He was born in Shrewsbury, Massachusetts, in 1877, the sole child of a poor farming couple. At age 14 he left home for a job; he earned $3 a week as a board marker at a Boston brokerage office.

From this modest start, and continuing through several years of apprenticeship trading odd lots at sundry bucket shops along the East Coast, this quiet, dedicated young man became one of the most feared and admired market operators during the first third of this century.

Livermore's universe was price fluctuations—both stock and commodity—and his obsession, the accurate projection of those prices. In fact, Edward J. Dies, one of the great financial commentators of that era, observed that, "should Livermore be shorn of every dollar, given a small brokerage credit, and locked in a room with tickers and phones, within a few active market months, he would reemerge with a new fortune."

From my earliest Wall Street days, starting in 1959, Livermore was my hero. And as I began developing some expertise in price analysis and trading, he became my coach and mentor in absentia. Like many investors, I've been influenced by his tactics, strategy and market philosophy.

"There is only one side of the market, and it is not the bull side or the bear side," he wrote, "but the right side."[1] That basic philosophy is indelibly etched in my mind, and I revert to it every time I read some lofty or tedious market analysis excessively focused on contentious argument rather than on practical market analysis and strategy.

Like most traders, I frequently face the decision of which positions to stick with and which to close out. And here, Livermore provides excellent, pinpoint counsel through a commentary describing his own mistakes. "I did precisely the wrong thing," he wrote. "The cotton showed me a loss and I kept it. The wheat showed me a profit and I sold it out. Of all the speculative blunders, there are few greater than trying to average a losing game. Always sell (close out) what shows you a loss and keep what shows you a profit." (Et tu, Livermore?)

However, Livermore's most significant legacy to investors concerns an overall strategy regarding investment objectives. It is particularly relevant during these times when traders are becoming increasingly dependent on powerful microcomputers and associated software. Even relatively inexperienced traders

---

[1] Edwin Lefevre, *Reminiscences of a Stock Operator* (Greenville, S.C.: Traders Press, 1923, republished 1985.)

are swinging in and out of sizable positions on the basis of tick-by-tick and on-line, short-term computerized chart presentations.

Pay heed to this piece of Livermore wisdom:

> After spending many years on Wall Street, and after making and losing millions of dollars, I want to tell you this. It never was my thinking that made the big money for me. It was my sitting. Got that? My sitting tight. It is no trick at all to be right on the market. You always find lots of early bulls in bull markets and lots of early bears in bear markets. I have known many men who were right at exactly the right time, and began buying or selling when prices were at the very level which should have made the greatest profit. And, their experience invariably matched mine. That is, they made no real money out of it. Men who can both be right and sit tight are uncommon. I found it one of the hardest things to learn. But it is only after a market operator has firmly grasped this that he can make big money. It is literally true that millions come easier to a trader after he knows how to trade, than hundreds did in the days of his ignorance.[2]

But perhaps the most significant of Livermore's considerable wisdom was contained in this quote (I have always felt that he wasn't just referring to market operations here—perhaps this is also a universal strategy for dealing in the game of life). "Losing money is the least of my troubles. A loss never bothers me after I take it. But being wrong—not taking the loss— that is what does the damage to the pocketbook and to the soul."[3]

Regrettably, my Florida fishing trip was much too short, and, about a week later, I was back in the frozen canyons of New York. While waiting for the big ones to affix themselves to my hook, I thought a lot about Livermore and his Florida fishing junkets, about his strategy and his considerable market wisdom. And, while his catch was undoubtedly more bountiful than my modest bunch of kingfish, I reveled in one advantage he couldn't possibly have had—I was able to study and enjoy his books and writings.

---

[2]Ibid.

[3]Ibid.

CHAPTER SEVENTEEN

The Market Is Neither Good Nor Bad

During much of the early 1980s, the tax shelter issue was of major concern to both the financial community and the federal government. On the one hand, the IRS and Congress focused on tightening or eliminating alleged loopholes. Indeed, the very heart of a huge tax-shelter industry was wiped out at one fell swoop with the signing of the Economic Recovery Act of 1981. Thus was ended the established practice, through tax straddles and subsequent rollovers, of an investor being able to convert short-term into long-term capital gains while deferring the tax liability by one or more years.

As a counterpoint, many in the financial community—commission firms, floor brokers, accountants and attorneys, and large investors—spent considerable time and money seeking ways to create new and viable shelters to replace those the government had voided.

But it was left to we commodity traders to unwittingly and unintentionally create a huge volume of perfectly legal, unassailable tax shelters. In fact, this type of shelter was so legitimate and straightforward, it hurt—literally! I'm talking about trading losses—losing money, and lots of it, by being on the wrong side of highly leveraged, fast-moving markets.

To this dubious list of tax shelter innovators, I must regretfully add my own name as well as the names of many of my colleagues, most of whom are professional operators with long years of established success. And we should have known better!

Isn't it curious that when an investor makes money, he attributes it to skill, superior acumen, and clever timing. But when he loses money—well, the market was terrible, too volatile, excessively choppy. We even hear such exculpations as world illiquidity, interest rate uncertainty, and massive government deficits. We might as well blame the phase of the moon or sunspots (don't snicker, some people do), the depth of trouser cuffs, or skirt hemlines.

Why can't we just admit that we were wrong in our perception of the market trend, our trade timing, or our tactical market approach. Only by acknowledging such pragmatism can we discover where and how we erred and how to avoid those mistakes the next time around.

The universal truth about futures markets is that, except for occasional and short-term aberrant periods, markets and price trends are not, in themselves, good or bad, right or wrong. It is the speculator himself who is good or bad or, more specifically, right or wrong. Throughout history, canny and successful speculators have repeatedly discovered this basic truism. And this commentary goes way back; the buying and selling of commodities have been linked with organized commerce for at least 50 centuries. Active commodity markets, under rules and regulations, existed in China, Egypt, Arabia, and India centuries before the advent of Christianity. Even in those days, the winners probably called the markets good and the losers called them bad.

And so, during this recent period, from mid-1983 to 1986, the markets were fine, thank you. It was the majority of speculators, commission firms, and advisory letters who were substantially wrong—on both the direction and the magnitude of the underlying major (down) trend of most markets. In succinct Americanese, we "zigged" (bought) when we should have "zagged" (sold). See Figure 17–1.

And, while the majority of traders had been playing the wrong (long) side of most futures and blaming their losses on "those crazy markets," the winners—those who had been playing the (down) trends in a disciplined and objective manner—were convinced that they were in some great markets. Same markets, folks—just the difference between being right and wrong.

In fact, during these choppy and random-appearing trends, with unexpected reversals and then reversals-from-reversals, it

FIGURE 17–1   CRB Futures Price Index (Long-Term Weekly Chart)
During the period mid-1983 to mid-1986, when markets were predominantly
down, most speculators were still playing long. Color their monthly statements
RED. The winners, who played the major (down) trend in an objective and
disciplined manner went home with all the winnings. Color their statements,
GREEN.

is more important than ever to play a disciplined and objective
game. We all get whipped around, but it is important that you
don't allow the market to upset or unnerve you. During early
1984, I got whipped in a big T bill position despite my best
resolutions to play by the rules. I had been short a line of September bills from February, held at a good profit, but was getting
pretty unnerved at the independent strength of the June bills.
Really strange, I thought to myself. I would have expected an
expiring-month squeeze in something like meats or one of the
grain markets. But in T bills? Anyway, the relentless strength of

the spot June future so undid me that I covered my entire line of short Septembers only to find, the very next day, that the market collapsed and the Septembers were down 20 points on the opening—and that's "only" $500 per contract. Too bad I didn't have my Buy the Strength and Sell the Weakness chapter at that time—it would have been very useful. But, worse than prematurely stopping out of a good short position, I was so bothered by my undisciplined play in bills that I missed a good buy signal on September 10 that resulted in a $5,500 move—and completely missed the entire profit!

During these difficult periods, there are lots of clear-thinking and disciplined technical traders whose accounts appreciate from 20 to 40 percent and that's not bad for these kind of years. One of the psychological problems that traders have to face, in terms of being right or wrong, is the subconscious reversal of two basic human emotions, *hope* and *fear*. Trader A is long beans in the direction of the major trend and is sitting with a profit. He sells on the first reaction *fearing* that if he continues to hold the position the market may reverse and he will lose his profit. Trader B, on the other hand, is short beans, against the major uptrend, and is sitting with a small but growing loss. He will sit with the losing position, *hoping* that the market will reverse its major trend (it probably won't, at least not while he's still short) and start moving south. In the meantime, the market continues in its major uptrend, and the loss continues to mount. What we have here are our principal emotions of *hope* and *fear*, but disoriented by 180 degrees. A, with his profitable, trending position in beans, should sit tight, *hoping* that the favorably moving market will continue to score profits for him. B, on the other hand, sitting with an unprofitable antitrend position, should close out, *fearing* that the adverse trend will continue (as it usually does) and the loss will continue to increase (it too, usually does).

Yet the contradictions abound, and a key element in successful trading is the way an operator reacts to both good and bad markets; that is, to winning and losing. Joe Klein, one of the best floor traders of his day whose successful career spanned more than 50 years in both the New York and Chicago pits, put it very succinctly. "Anyone can be a hero when he's long a big line and the market is moving sharply higher, with some limit-bid days thrown in. But the mark of a true professional is how he plays when he is behind; when the market is going against him and he can't seem to regain his balance or his equilibrium."

And Joe Klein should know. In contrast to today's leading floor traders who tend to concentrate on a single pit or exchange floor, Klein was the perennial traveler. During the 1940s through the 60s, he kept an overnight bag under his desk in a small office at the Cotton Exchange. So equipped, he was ready to move with the action. If the bean or wheat market started jumping and Joe's charts told him that he ought to play them seriously, he would grab his bag, hail a cab for LaGuardia Airport, and get on the next flight to the Windy City. And the Chicago boys wouldn't be the least surprised to see Joe Klein step into the bean pit the following morning; after all, that's where the action was.

What does Joe Klein's statement about winning and losing really mean? The true test of how expert or professional an operator is—and this just as applicable in any other field or profession—is the way the operator handles the bad times. I've seen many high-flying speculators, who had amassed substantial paper fortunes by getting on the right side of a dynamic one-way market (invariably heading north), lose their bundle and then some when the market turned south. The mark of the true professional is his staying power—his ability to weather the inevitable adversities and come out on top.

It is only human, of course, to become discouraged when trading goes badly. When, despite your best intentions and attempts at an objective and disciplined approach, just about every trade seems to turn bad. We all have times like these. I've found that the best thing to do when such moments arise is to walk away from the market for as long as it takes to get your head cleared and your attitude positive. The market will be there when you return. I am reminded of a story told about Dickson Watts, a famous old cotton trader from the 19th century. When asked for advice by a trader who claimed that the size of his position kept him awake at night, Watts' reply was direct and on target: "Sell down to a sleeping level." Have you ever been unable to sleep because of your futures position? Have you ever sold down to a sleeping level?

CHAPTER EIGHTEEN

You Must Control and Limit Your Losses

Futures traders would do well to reflect on a statement made by Chicago-based Richard Dennis, acknowledged as the most successful of today's big operators. *The majority of his profits come from just 5 percent of his trades.* And, don't forget, we are talking about telephone number-size profits.

Most speculators depend on an array of mechanical and computerized gadgets to help them in their trend identification and trade timing. They spend a lot of time squinting at price screens and price charts that run the gamut from simple line or point and figure, to multidimensional moving-average combinations and exotic concoctions like RSI, DM, square of R, etc. There are even those quick-action, on-line tick charts the operator can preset for anywhere from 30- or 60-minute bar intervals right down to 5- or even 3-minute intervals.

But perhaps I can coax you away, if only briefly, from those paper and electronic aids and suggest that you focus on the significance of Mr. Dennis's intriguing statement—that the majority of his profits come from just 5 percent of his trades.

Exactly how Mr. Dennis develops his trend identification and trade timing are not necessarily germane to this discussion—besides, his methods are proprietary and understandably kept secret. But what is not secret is that he obviously views sound money management and trading strategy to be every bit as im-

portant as his charting or computer technique. This is something
that most of us can stand to take some lessons on.

Before the proliferation of the microcomputer and the availability of powerful software, traders had to rely on their experience and recall and on their ability to study and interpret price
charts or fundamental data. Often the decision-making process
depended on things like instinct, intuition, or plain gut feeling.
The successful operators managed to synthesize a "chemistry"
combining these subjective skills with a technical expertise. And
their bottom-line results over any period of time depended on the
sum of the above factors combined with each one's particular
approach to money management and investment strategy.

Each of the players developed his own style and approach.
These were as varied as the number of serious practitioners.
Strategies ranged from, "Don't put all your eggs in one basket"
(diversify with a balanced array of six, eight, or even more markets) to Baruch's oft-quoted dictum to "Put all your eggs in one
basket but watch the basket carefully." In fact, before my 1975
"retirement," I characteristically put all or most of my eggs into
one basket, whether the basket contained copper, wheat, or
sugar. On occasion, this approach paid off very handsomely.

Without question, a key to Mr. Dennis's success, as well as to
the success of all the leading operators, is their ability to curb
losses—to keep them within acceptable limits. OK, you might
ask, what is an acceptable limit in which to hold my losses? My
first response would be for you to keep *all* paper losses within your
personal sleeping level. Obviously, once any loss on an open
position reaches the point where it affects your sleep, your job
performance, or your personal life, it has reached the "excessive"
level and should be reduced or liquidated. That's not all there is to
say on that subject, however. I have seen countless individuals
who spend hours at automobile dealerships trying to save a few
hundred on a new car sit with paper losses in the thousands
without flinching. Obviously, we must arrive at some objective,
pragmatic understanding of when to pull the plug on an adverse
position. At the outset, I will say that the least intelligent way of
deciding when to quit a losing position is how the trader feels
about its viability. It makes little difference if he thinks it has
profit potential or is hopeless and should be abandoned or even

closed out and reversed. Hardly any trader, professional or otherwise, is even remotely qualified to make this determination because that would presuppose the ability to predict next week's or next month's prices. And no one can do that. Let's make the decision entirely objective! One way to do this would be to equate allowable risk on any position with the respective exchange margin. For instance, you could limit your loss to, say, 50 or 100 percent of the margin. Furthermore, once the position shows a good profit of, say, 50 percent of the margin, you start advancing the stop by some preset formula. There is a compelling rationale to this approach. The amount of margin, as established by each exchange for its commodities, is generally related to the price level and the trading volatility of each market; hence, indirectly to its profit potential.

For example, you would risk twice as much on a wheat position as on a corn position—the exchange margin is $750 versus $400. And I would project the price volatility of wheat to be double that of corn.

There is another good reason for setting stops this way. You want to keep them away from the accumulation of stops at the so-called logical chart points used by the majority of commission house speculators. These popular stop points frequently serve as targets for trade firms and big locals to shoot at. The May 1987 coffee future serves as an example. Coffee had been in a major bear market since topping out at the 2.60 level in late 1985. From June through September 1986, the downtrend took a pause and traded generally sideways, between 1.65 and 2.00. By late August, a large concentration of buy stops had accumulated just above 2.00 on a closing basis. This fact did not escape the attention of the large professional operators. Accordingly, during the week of September 22, the market experienced a "sudden" surge of heavy professional buying, putting values up to 2.07. Oops—there went all the speculative buy stops. Following this cleaning out of the stops and the reversal to long of many trading systems and speculative positions, the buying "suddenly" abated. Next, heavy professional selling "suddenly" hit the floor. Not unexpectedly, the market resumed its major downtrend, with values plummeting down to the 1.00 level. This was the classic bear trap (see Figure 18−1).

FIGURE 18−1   May 1987 Coffee

Here was the classic bear trap. During a three-month sideways (1.65−2.00) respite in an ongoing major bear market, the trade noted a large concentration of speculative short positions in the market with buy stops just above 2.00. Not surprisingly, during the week of September 22, the market experienced a "sudden" surge of heavy professional buying, taking out all the buy stops and reversing the trending systems and the speculative positions to long. After the buy stops had been cleaned out, the buying "suddenly" abated, and heavy professional selling "suddenly" hit the market. Values plummeted clear down to the 1.00 level.

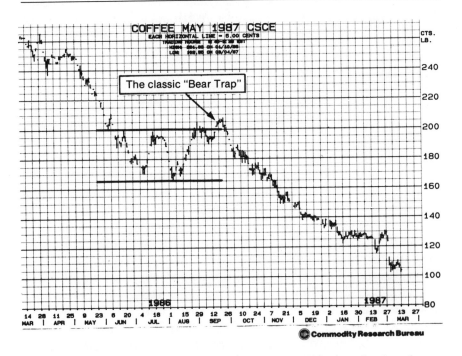

Another Chicago professional is Robert Moss, who has been associated with C and D Commodities on the floor of the Board of Trade. Here is what Moss says about his operating strategy.

- Let profits run and don't worry about taking them. Worry about minimizing losses.
- On any given trade, I would not want to lose more than 4 percent of the capital invested.
- Of my trades, 5 to 8 percent are profitable, 10 percent are breakeven, and the rest are losers.

- I tend to make money two days out of five, break even another two days, and have losses one day.

There are other compelling reasons why the operator must control his losses as well as his overall trading activity, and they relate to the cost of doing business. First of all, you pay a commission whether you win or lose. Let's say your commission cost is $50 per round turn. A profit of $500 nets out at $450, while a loss of $500 nets down to $550. In fact, I've seen many active traders whose annual commission bills have run to nearly 100 percent of their starting equity. They would have to make a 100 percent trading profit in every year just to break even. Food for thought, isn't it? Secondly, it is far more difficult to make up losses than it is to lose in the first place. Take a trader who starts with $30,000 and who loses $10,000, equal to 33 percent of his capital. He is now down to $20,000, and, in order to get back to his $30,000 beginning equity, he must increase his account by $10,000—for a 50 percent appreciation. He loses 33 percent but must make back 50 percent to come out whole. And it's even worse because of the commission costs, which are charged on both profitable and losing trades. You might try working out some other percentage combinations of losing versus winning—it doesn't make for entertaining reading.

A number of years ago, while formulating certain trading strategies, I did a survey of my clients' trading over the years. The results were generally unimpressive, which should not have been surprising. Then I restructured just one aspect of their trading, calculating what the results would have been if losses had been limited by some objective formula to, say, 45 percent of the respective margins. Without exception, the results were substantially improved: I took into consideration those positions that were closed on this "45 percent rule" but that subsequently reversed and would have resulted in profits had they not been liquidated on such a close stop. Judge for yourself:

1. A New England metals fabricator invested $105,000 in a trading account, and after nine months had lost its original capital plus an additional $30,000. A recap of its activity revealed a total of 35 trades, of which 12 were profitable and 23 were not. That was not the problem— its Waterloo was that the average size profit was $1,799

per contract while the average loss was $6,844. Terrible, wasn't it? If this firm had limited its losses to 45 percent of margin for each position, it would have suffered an overall loss of just $9,232 instead of the $135,000 it actually lost. Its average size loss would have been $1,340 per contract instead of $6,844. Some difference!

2.   And, lest you think that big losses only happen to public traders, here is the trading record of an otherwise highly sophisticated private European bank whose trader used to TELEX me orders for execution in Chicago and New York. Starting capital was $100,000. After 13 months it had been depleted to $54,500, at which time the bank discharged its local trader and quit speculative operations. During those 13 months only 3 of their 14 trades were profitable. Their average size profit was a dismal $255 per contract, while their average size loss was $4,156. Isn't that incredible? Had the bank limited its losses to 45 percent of margins and permitted its profits to run until taken out by the stops, its overall loss would have been a mere $6,719 ($634 per contract), and it could have continued trading till it caught some good trends and moved into profitability.

3.   It is enlightening to compare these two traders' results with that of a small trading fund that started with just $18,000. After 18 months of operations, its capital had appreciated to $130,000. Of its total 230 trades, 150 were profitable. Of greater significance, the average size profit was $1,020 per contract, while the average loss was kept to $515.

These recaps tell the story, and the conclusions are inescapable. Traders 1 and 2 traded against the major trends and made no serious attempt to limit losses on adverse positions. On the contrary, profitable positions were quickly closed out, while losses were allowed to develop into even bigger losses. The trading fund, on the other hand, exercised the considerable discipline of trading with the prevailing major trends, following a strict policy of minimizing losses and allowing profits to run. They played by the rules, and their bottom line reflects it.

Why You Should Cut Your Losses and Let Your Profits Run

	Metals Fabricator	European Bank	Private Pool
Starting capital	$105,000	$100,000	$ 18,000
Net profit (loss)	($135,000)	($ 45,500)	$112,000
Percent profitable trades	34%	21%	65%
Average size profit	$ 1,799	$ 255	$ 1,020
Average size loss	$ 6,844	$ 4,156	$ 515
Average size loss if limited to 45 percent of margin	$ 1,340	$ 634	—
Total net loss if limited to 45 percent of margin	$ 9,232	$ 6,719	—

In terms of controlling and limiting losses, many experienced operators have likened trading strategy to particular aspects of chess strategy. For instance, the chess player has to be prepared to lose certain pieces in order to gain some tactical advantage or to capture some other piece of even greater value. What chess player wouldn't be willing to sacrifice a bishop or rook in order to capture his opponent's queen? The speculative corollary is that you must be prepared to sacrifice your antitrend losing positions in favor of your with-the-trend winning positions. There is no valid logic in holding onto and defending these losing positions when, with the same funds, you can defend or add to your with-the-trend profitable positions. Another chess strategy that is applicable to speculative operations is that white plays to win while black plays for a draw. What does this mean? In a game between two equally ranked masters, white moves first and is assumed to have the advantage. He therefore pursues an aggressive stance aimed at victory. Black, on the other hand, is assumed to be starting at a disadvantage and normally takes a defensive posture at the outset. Unless white carelessly commits some tactical faux pas that would pass the advantage to black, black maintains this defensive stance. He is content to play to a draw, looking forward to taking an aggressive and win-oriented strategy in a subsequent game where he plays white and has the first move.

How does this analogy relate to trading strategy? On your

with-the trend holdings—analogous to the first move in chess—you have the dominant position and play an aggressive game for a big win. Here you hold for the major move, rather than close out quickly for a small profit. However, when you are sitting with an against-the-trend position—the second move in chess—you assume a defensive posture and content yourself with a draw or a breakeven closeout if you can get one. Here it makes little sense to try to sit it out, hoping that the trend will flip to favor your adverse position and offer you a big score on the trade. If you can finesse a breakeven trade, take it. You have a far greater chance of making your money on with-the-trend positions than on those adverse, wishful-thinking situations.

I experienced this strategy first hand in the Swiss franc market in late 1986. Swiss had been in a strong downtrend until March (see Figure 18–2) when it got down to the 51.00 level (basis December future). It then turned north. And what a bull deal it was, with values advancing all the way to 62.00 by early October. I had been long on two occasions, having dumped the most recent position just above 61.00 on what appeared to be a grossly overbought technical situation. It was still a strong uptrend and a bull market, I reasoned, so I just sat on the sidelines awhile, waiting to reenter the long side on a sharp reaction.

But where to place the buy orders? I projected good buying support around 59.00 (basis December) at the double-bottom support level and waited for what I hoped would be the inevitable technical reaction. I didn't have long to wait. On October 27, the market dropped into my buying zone, and I loaded up. My euphoria lasted a whole two days with a 100-point rally, but I hadn't reckoned with "them," who must have just discovered that I had been buying and who were waiting to clobber me. Just six days later, I was sitting with a 100-point loss ($1,250 per contract on a large position) and in a market that had taken out all logical support and now appeared poised to commence a fullbore retreat. What a shock! I realized that I was suddenly afflicted with the futures trader's recurring malady—egg on the face.

Over the next couple of days, the "what's going on?" phone calls from a number of anxious clients served to remind me that I had better find a viable means of dealing with this situation. I reverted to my one reliable mainstay—my "drawing board" of short- and long-term charts and the trend-following computer

FIGURE 18−2   December 1986 Swiss Franc

During the week of November 3, the market smashed through support at the 59.00 double-bottom level, breaking the uptrend line and flipping the technical systems to short. The reaction found support at the 58.00 level, and, on the ensuing rally, I dumped my long position around 59.50. I was now out of the market.

Following this market break, values reversed back to north, and the technical indicators signaled the new uptrend on December 19. It was a timely call; following expiration of the December future, there was still another 800 points on the upside.

SWISS FRANC DEC 1986 IMM

EACH HORIZONTAL LINE = .0050 DOLLARS
TRADING HOURS: 8: 20-2: 16 EST
HIGH: .6268 ON 09/19/86
LOW: .4885 ON 12/18/85

Commodity Research Bureau

system that I had been using for nearly four years. No doubt about it, the trend had clearly turned down. The overriding sentiment was decidedly bearish. The market was down to the 58.00 level, which coincided with a 40 percent downward retracement of the previous up-leg, and I projected some sort of a technical bounce from this support area. My strategy was to sit through this down-leg, to assume we would get some sort of a rally off the 58.00 level, and, if possible, to dump the entire position into resistance around 59.50.

This would mean a breakeven trade. What kind of a strategy, one might ask, has as its objective the closeout of a big position at a breakeven point? Why wouldn't I prefer to make a profit on it? Of course I would prefer to make a profit—but it didn't seem to be in the cards, and here's why. Although I try to play my positions only in the direction of the ongoing major trend, it's not always possible due to the dynamic nature of these volatile markets. Besides, you may enter a position with the trend, only to see it reverse after you are aboard. Under those circumstances, it is best to get out of the position as quickly as possible to minimize your loss. If you are able to walk away with a breakeven, so much the better. There is always the chance that, shortly after you liquidate, the market will reverse back to its original direction and you will have closed out unnecessarily. But that's one of the risks of the game, and you learn to live with it. Besides, if you see that you have exited prematurely, you can try to reenter with a clear head and at a more favorable opportunity. The odds favor profits on your with-the-trend positions, and that's where you should focus your attention and your funds.

My Swiss franc position was now against the trend, and the market had penetrated both the uptrend line and the 59.00 support level—hence the decision to dump. And since I projected a likely rally back into the 59.50 resistance level, it would serve as my sell point. That notwithstanding, I had a below-the-market stop, around 57.40, as my bailout point in case the rally fizzled. On November 10 and 11, Swiss rallied up into my sell zone, and I did just that. Chalk up one breakeven trade. Was I concerned that the market would again flip to up and advance to new highs? Not in the least. I played it just the way I should have considering the circumstances. As a boy, I recall reading a quote by Satchel Paige, one of baseball's great early pitchers. "Don't look back—someone might be gaining on you." In fact, following this November break-even liquidation, the market did flip back to a strong bull trend. Attentive technical traders had the opportunity to get back aboard the long side, as many of the trading systems signaled a buy on December 19.

There is an old Scottish saying, "You mind your pennies and the pounds will take care of themselves." Perhaps the speculative corollary is, "You mind your losses and the profits will take care of themselves."

The Thrill of Catching the Mega-Move

There may be some traders who can get all excited about the prospects of a month-long rally in yen or Swiss francs or a move in GNMAs or some other alphabet-soup assortment of financial futures. And I'll concede that, as pragmatic traders, we focus on dollars and not on excitement or emotions. It shouldn't much matter if we make our big money in soybeans or jellybeans. The important thing is that we make the big profits. That notwithstanding, all these financial futures combined can't generate the kind of sheer raw excitement, the hold-your-breath roller coaster-like thrill of a big move in soybeans!

My first major play on Wall Street occurred in soybeans—the 1961 bull deal in Chicago. This market had all the ingredients to impress a freshman Merrill Lynch account executive recently arrived from the firm's six-month training program. And, although Merrill had spent a small fortune teaching me all aspects of the financial business, the rest of the *products* in my sales kit paled by comparison with the action in futures. I knew that I was hooked when I found myself walking into the corner office of Sam Mothner, my office manager and mentor, reintroducing myself as, "your new commodity specialist." A brief discussion ensued in which he did most of the discussing! He tried to talk me out of this crazy notion. But I was adamant, and he was sufficiently experienced to realize that his new 27-year-old account executive was very committed. I was thrilled when I left his office some 20 minutes later as the new commodity specialist.

Over the years, I've made it a point to get to Chicago for a day or two on the floor each time there was a boiling soybean market. I never tire of witnessing this spectacle, perhaps the most exciting floor action on any exchange. On one memorable occasion, I watched in awe as a young floor broker from one of the commission firms entered the bean pit with a large buy order during a violent price reaction. The market seemed to be plummeting into a black hole, and his was the only bid in the pit at that moment. The action was fast and furious, and the young broker bought his million-or-so beans in record time. Seconds later, he staggered down the littered steps of the bean pit to the relative quiet and security of his firm's telephone booth. His trader's floor jacket had been slightly altered by the crowd of sellers who had descended on him like piranhas. There he was, still in a slight daze, *minus his two jacket sleeves.* They had been wrenched right off his limp jacket by several screaming and gesticulating colleagues eager to help the young broker buy all the beans they were trying to sell. I'll never forget that day—I'll bet he won't either.

In 1975, after 16 years in the front-line trenches of futures trading, I had been in more than my share of big moves—for big profits *and* big losses. I'd made a few killings and had been the victim of quite a few. They ran the gamut from agriculturals and meats to softs and metals. I was 41 years old, had attained my goals, both personal and financial, and felt that I needed a long and leisurely break. So I took a five-year sabbatical, during which I studied, wrote, and traveled. I tried to avoid thinking of the markets altogether. But any time I heard of big action in beans, I felt a quickening of the pulse, a flush of the temple, and a twinge of anxiety. This stuff gets into your blood.

In August of 1983, back on Wall Street, I ventured to Chicago for my personal homage to King Bean. The market had, once again, confounded the experts by soaring through the roof at a totally unexpected time. There had been a modest rally from January through April, punctuated by a brief reactionary pause during February (there's the February break again). The April advance stalled at 7.20 (basis March 1984 future) and then collapsed into a 10-week slide right down to new contract lows around 6.20. A bear market shaping up, right? Wrong! Following this big break, around the first week in July, the bean market commenced a modest advance lasting just 11 weeks. It carried values up to 9.90 for a whopping move of over $18,000 on just $1,500 margin. Talk about big moves and megaprofits! And, during that bull move, especially above the 9.00 level, the rallying cry among the Chicago bean watchers was "beans in the teens." Well, it didn't quite make that level; the market topped out just short of $10.00 (basis March future) and spent the next several years in full retreat (see Figure 19–1).

If you get the feeling that soybean watchers start chanting, whistling, and stomping every time they see a 40- or 60-cent rally, looking for another $2 or more, you're absolutely right. Matter of fact, they are joined in their "bull dance" by a consortium of mostly Midwest merchants who deal in luxury tangibles such as homes and apartments, boats, cars, and jewelry. A bull move in soybeans, with its vast public and professional participation,

---

FIGURE 19–1 March 1984 Soybeans
The market once again confounded the soybean watchers by soaring through the roof following a collapse to the 6.20 level in early July. Talk about dynamic moves. This bull deal advanced from 6.20 to 9.90, a move of some $18,000 per contract, in just three months. Although the Chicago boys kept chanting, "beans in the teens," they never quite made it to double digits. The next three years were spent with the soybean market in full retreat.

SOYBEANS MAR. 1984 - CHI.
EACH HORIZONTAL LINE = 10 CENTS

CONTRACT COMPLETED
MARCH 21, 1984
HIGH 993 1/2   LOW 616

Commodity Research Bureau

typically creates more new millionaires and solidifies more existing ones over a relatively brief period of time than a major move in any other commodity. Regrettably, quite a few of these instant millionaires fall off the ride when the market turns south and prices plummet even faster than the original rally. Anyone in the market for a pre-owned yacht, limousine, Rolex watch, or Chicago lakeside condo should coordinate his purchase with the final stages of a bull market washout in soybeans.

Hardly any futures trader needs to be convinced about these two points: *(a)* If you're lucky or skillful enough to catch the top or bottom of a market that develops into a major move, *and* if you're lucky or skillful enough to stick with the position for the majority of the move, *and* if you're lucky or skillful enough to limit losses on your other positions, you're going to make a lot of money. *(b)* If you make a lot of money, as in *(a)* above, you're going to have one hell of a time spending it. Any dissenters? I can give firsthand personal testimony verifying these two truths.

Clearly, the issue is not how to spend the big winnings. We can all figure out how to do that. Rather, it's how to snare the big winnings. You can't do it on the basis of market gossip, tips, or because you may have lost money on your last 5 or 10 campaigns and the law of averages now favors you as a winner. To make a big score, your best bet is a disciplined and carefully calculated long-term campaign with a strategic plan guiding the entire operation.

How about luck as an ally? You might win one tennis or chess game due to luck. But can you imagine winning a major tennis or chess tournament, covering quite a few contests, on the basis of luck? I hardly think so. Likewise with futures, you need a well-organized and detailed strategic plan covering all contingencies, executed in a pragmatic and disciplined manner.

As an example of a detailed strategic battle plan, I would like to share with you the strategic plan that I prepared in early 1987 for dealing with the silver market. Objective: megaprofits or modest losses. Such a plan, covering the various aspects detailed below, should be structured for every major position you take for the big move.

The major trend is still down, with long-term support likely between 5.00 and 5.50 and overhead resistance toward the 8.00 level (see Figure 19−2). The intermediate trend, on the other hand, is sideways, and I project buying support on reactions

FIGURE 19−2 Long-Term Weekly (Nearest Future) Silver
The major trend is down, and the intermediate trend is sideways. The market
should find long-term buying support on reactions toward the 5.00−5.50 level. A
close over 6.50 (nearest future) should turn the intermediate trend to up, and
a close over 7.10 should turn the major trend to up.

towards 5.00 and resistance around 6.00, at 6.50 and again at 7.00,
basis nearest future weekly close.

So how to play this market? For anyone willing and able to
stand the considerable financial and emotional risks, the significant play could be from the long side. Since making its major top
at 14.00 in early 1983, the market has retreated to deep within a
substantial long-term base area and, following an extended side-

ways consolidation period, should ultimately pop out of this area on the upside.

The key word here is *ultimately*. It's hard enough to project *where* a market will go—but *when* is virtually impossible. In fact, it's in the pursuit of the elusive *when* that so many traders, including experienced professionals, come to grief. To put this in perspective, we have only to look at the many bullish silver studies and trade recommendations that bombarded us during 1985. Yet the market registered life-of-contract lows during first-half 1986—making a hash out of every one of those impressive bullish advisories.

How would I play this silver market? I would start with the premise that it is virtually impossible to accurately predict where silver or any other market will be trading at any future time. My strategy, then, is to structure a series of consecutive tactical moves in which I advance to each stage only after each previous stage has performed according to the scenario. This method should minimize the excessive risks of the operation, controlling them to an acceptable degree.

The opening stage in my strategy is to begin accumulating a long silver position toward the long-term 5.00−5.50 (basis nearest future) support area. Now, assuming that this support level holds—and at this early stage in the operation we have no assurance that it will—we then move to the second stage; that is, we buy an additional silver increment on a weekly close (nearest future) above 6.50. Assuming the market continues to follow this generally bullish scenario, we buy a third increment on a weekly close (again, nearest future) above 7.10. At that point, I would project that the intermediate trend had turned up on the 6.50 close and also the major trend on the 7.10 close.

My *price projection* for the move? Should the market follow my scenario, I would expect an initial price objective of 6.80−7.00 (basis nearest future, weekly close) with an intermediate objective further down the line in the 9.50−10.50 range. Regarding any long-term price projection—it's just too early to think about that at this time. My *time projection* for the move? From four months to two years. Actually, the time projection is the least exact and least relevant aspect of this analysis. Obviously, patience is a clear requisite to play this game.

Despite the foregoing, we must acknowledge that the major trend is still sideways to down. Accordingly, the odds still favor a continuation of the ongoing bear trend. In essence, we are trying to bottom-pick within a strongly entrenched bear market, and that's no easy task. Clearly, at this indeterminate stage, this is not a selection for the faint of heart or purse.

That's all that need be said about the strategy at this point with one exception. What if the market heads south, instead of north the way it's supposed to go? Have you heard the one about the professional speculator who lost $18,000 *per contract* on a big long silver position a few years ago? I have because I was his broker—and he's the one who waited to buy until he knew that the big boys were in there buying. Big boys notwithstanding, this silver market is one helluva fast and leveraged game, and the stakes are high. So, unless you are a first-class masochist or have an uncontrollable desire to get a genuine tax loss named in your honor, you'd better have a bailout plan ready. That translates into a stop-loss point to take you out at your personal pain threshold, perhaps around the $1,200 to $2,000 per contract loss limit. And, if you get stopped out, you might take another shot at the long side on a further decline to the 4.00 to 5.00 level. Adhere to the rest of the scenario by adding to the position in increments with the on-close buy stops.

That's my long-range strategic plan for silver, prepared in February of 1987. Let's examine some of its particulars:

1. The most obvious aspect is that the major trend is sideways to down and I am looking to buy the market—a violation of trend-trading dogma. However, the intermediate trend is sideways, and two of the long-term early warning systems that I follow have flashed buy signals for silver. Moreover, the market has achieved its downside count and has fallen into an area of strong long-term technical support around the 5.00 level. And I do have efficient stops under the position that would limit losses in the event the downtrend continues.
2. Will the downtrend continue? I have no idea. If it does, I'm out of the market with a modest loss. If it turns up, out of the long-term base area, this step-by-step strategic sce-

nario could result in exceptional gains. I would project that the profit potential is greater than the risk by a sufficient multiple, making the play worthwhile.

3. Is this scenario for the average trader? Probably not. It's a particularly high-risk high-reward play and only for those who understand and can accept the high stakes involved. A large measure of patience and discipline will be needed to handle this long-term campaign, which could take as long as two years to work out.

In case this strategic scenario sounds a little too complex or difficult for you to engineer, is there some other way to score megaprofits? Consider the experience of some 400 commodity traders scattered throughout the world. The computerized print-out from their long-term trading system, which I monitor daily, flashed a buy signal on coffee, October 10, 1985, at a price of 139.93 (basis the perpetual price, equivalent to a 91-day future). What was so remarkable about that? Nothing yet. The system remained long about 16 weeks, till January 29, 1986, when it put out a sell signal. The price? 223.34. And, if you have to ask what was so remarkable about that, you ought to brush up on your elementary arithmetic. The difference between 139.93 and 223.34 is 83.41 cents, and at $375 per cent, the move amounted to "just" over $31,000 *per contract* (see Figure 19–3). Here was a mega-move, without any doubt!

It's obvious that this was not your normal, everyday trading profit. However, some successful long-term technical traders and trading systems out there are able to score a number of big profits annually—and I define a big profit as anything around or over $5,000 per contract. Moreover, lots of other traders do manage to get aboard these markets somewhere near the inception of the move. Regrettably, though, they don't also manage to remain aboard for the duration or even a major portion of it. Anyone who has been trading for at least a few years will surely recall positions he had that, if held for the extent of the move, would have resulted in a megaprofit. The key phrase here is, "if held for the extent of the move," because it rarely is. I reinvite your attention to the Livermore quote in Chapter 16, paraphrased in part here: "You always find lots of early bulls in bull markets and lots of

FIGURE 19-3 May 1986 Coffee
Over 400 system traders throughout the world got a buy signal at 139.93 on
October 10, 1985, and a subsequent sell signal at 223.34 on January 29, 1986
(prices basis 91-day perpetual). The profit on the trade was 83.41 cents, equal
to over $31,000 per contract. These occasional megaprofits more than cover
the losses posted by long-term position systems when they are whipsawed
by broad, sideways markets.

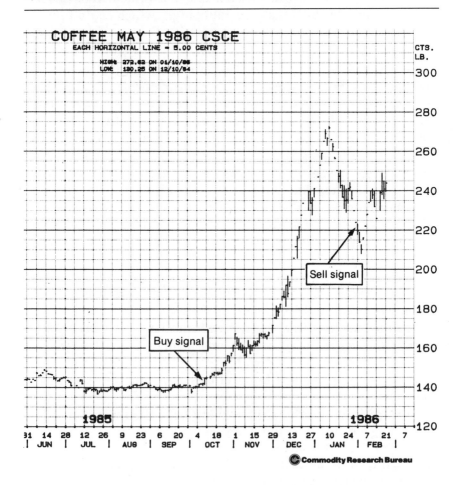

early bears in bear markets. . . . They made no real money out of
it. . . . Men who can both be right and sit tight are uncommon."

We obviously have no way of knowing, when we put on a
position, if it will turn into the big one. Therefore, so long as we

are trading in the direction of the major trend, we should premise that *every* position has the potential to be the megamove and play the market accordingly. And that means holding the position ("sitting tight," as Livermore would say) until your stop, which you advance with the market, takes you out. One of the best examples of a totally unexpected megamove was in cotton. On August 13, 1986, traders in some of the long-term trading systems got what appeared to be a routine buy signal in cotton, at 34.54 (prices basis perpetual price). The signal appeared a little dubious, especially because the market had been locked into a huge bear trend from the 68.00 level with cotton traders having spilled lots of red ink while bottom-probing during past months. In fact, many experienced cotton traders were weary from successive losses on antitrend long positions and opted to sit this one out. Meanwhile, most of the neophytes, believing the admonition in their systems manuals to "take *all* signals," followed the signal and bought the cotton.

I don't think that anyone was more amazed than I was at what actually happened. On the afternoon of January 28, 1987, some 5½ months after the buy position was signaled, I received a near-cryptic phone call from a pharmacist in Rapid City, South Dakota. He and I had corresponded on occasion, and, if there ever was a rank beginner in futures trading, he was it. Anyway, he was so excited he could barely talk—but the gist of what I understood, after I managed to get him to communicate in normal English, was that his system just that morning had flashed a signal, at 54.83, to sell the cotton position. He had dumped the position and was totally undone at the realization that he had just scored over $20,000 profit on his two contracts. After further conversation, I was also undone when I learned that he had been unaware until that very day of the magnitude of his profit— which may have been the reason he sat with it for the full term of the move (see Figure 19–4).

No doubt about it, this gentleman from South Dakota experienced the Thrill of Catching the Big Move for the Megaprofit. And you can too, once you begin operating with a consistent discipline to trade the moving markets in the direction of the major trend, to stick with the position till your (advancing) stop takes you out, and to resist excessive positioning or overtrading due to boredom, tips, or market gossip.

FIGURE 19–4   July 1987 Cotton

Following a virtually uninterrupted downtrend from the 68.00 level, system traders received their long-awaited buy signal on August 13, 1986. The long position was held for 5½ months and was liquidated on a sell signal on January 28, 1987. The profit was some $10,000 per contract. Here is another example of a megaprofit generated by a position trading system in a dynamically trending market. But the same system that produced this profit produces a succession of losses during broad sideways markets.

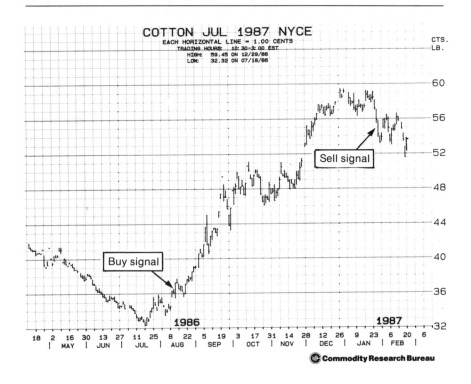

COTTON JUL 1987 NYCE

_____

The Market Doesn't Take Prisoners

It was my annual tour of the New York Boat Show. My son and I paused for a brief rest after two hours of traipsing the aisles and booths of the various exhibitors, and I couldn't help overhearing an animated conversation nearby. There was a terrific baseball movie that, according to this group's consensus should not be missed. The movie was *The Natural*, and, being a former baseball fan, I rented it for my VCR the following weekend. It really was a terrific film—about personal courage and commitment, patience, discipline, and the importance of a high standard of excellence. Oh yes, it was also about baseball. I've thought about this film and what it meant to different viewers. Was it a baseball film? Undeniably yes. But from my perspective, that was the least important aspect of the story. The importance of commitment, discipline, self-confidence, and courage were, for me, what it was all about.

The parallels to futures trading are unmistakable, albeit not so obvious. When I first got involved with these markets in the early 1960s, my outlook was straightforward, bordering on the simplistic. I studied charting technique, spent hours learning to recognize top and bottom formations with all sorts of esoteric names, and endlessly debated the accuracy of projecting price moves with line versus point-and-figure counts. The strategies of speculation or hedging, the principles of sound money management, and the personal and emotional traits needed to be a winner were scribbled on a couple of small index cards. I kept one in my calendar book, another in my top desk drawer, and a third in my shirt pocket for ready reference. Like other traders, I tended to focus on the technical aspects of markets and trading, relegating strategies and tactics to a distinctly secondary niche.

From the vantage point of some 30 years I can see that the balance shifted gradually, but unmistakably, to a near 50:50 formula between technical and strategic considerations. I've often remarked that, if forced to choose between a first-class technical system with average strategies and tactics or an average technical system with outstanding strategies and tactics, I would opt for the latter every time. It is the strategy and tactics, the money management and emotional control that has absorbed my interest generally for 15 or 20 years—particularly during the five years I've been writing this book. It will absorb you during the time that you read it and, hopefully, for long after you put it back on the shelf.

My own trading, over the course of these years, has run the gamut from very good to very bad—from very profitable to near-disastrous. Without a doubt, though, my biggest profits and most comfortable positions have occurred when I was trading in the direction of the prevailing major trend. Conversely, my biggest losses and greatest stresses (for they seem to travel hand-in-hand), occurred when I took or sat with antitrend positions held at losses. This is unquestionably the universal experience. It applies to seasoned professional and rank neophyte, to speculators and hedgers. It applies to operators in New York, Chicago, London, Zurich, and Hong Kong.

I've been fortunate enough to have experienced the mind-boggling sensation of taking seven-figures-to-the-left-of-the-decimal-point profits and six-figures-to-the-left-of-the-decimal-point losses. Fortunate to have taken losses? Yes indeed—because we learn more, or at least we ought to, from our losses than from our profits. But, as someone once said, "I've had profits and I've had losses, and profits are better."

A colleague recently remarked that, after all these years, I seem to have retained a sense of humor about the business. That may be true, and a sense of humor is unquestionably an asset in any field of endeavor. But for the futures trader, having a sense of humor goes hand-in-hand with having a balanced perspective.

You need it to get you through the inevitable ups and downs (the "oops" periods) in this wild and woolly business.

The seasoned operator has learned from long and costly experience that he is going to encounter good periods, when he is emotionally very *up,* and bad periods, when his spirits sink like lead weights. He truly needs a good sense of emotional balance and market perspective. He must ride out those good times and not get seduced by sudden success; and he must avoid getting carried away (or carried out) during the bad times.

Disappointment and discouragement are two basic human emotions. The serious operator must have the self-discipline to overcome the blues and to stick with an objective, systematic method of futures investing. Of no less importance, he must maintain the self-confidence to be able to plow through the bad days (or weeks or months) because that is the only way to make the losses back, with interest, during the next good period. And, no matter how grim things may appear, there will definitely be a "next good period" so long as the operator stays alive by limiting losses on adverse positions.

Another way of saying this was articulated by a gentleman named Dennis Conner in 1987. Mr. Conner may not know very much about the specifics of futures trading, but he has to be one of the world's leading experts on winning and losing. To him fell the dubious distinction of being the only U.S. America's Cup helmsman to lose the cup in the long history of that competition, only to win it back in 1987 with four straight victories. "It is not how you get hit, but how you recover," he uttered. And he should know!

Anyone writing a book of an instructional nature runs a certain risk. There is bound to be some fellow who, after reading the book, will break all the rules, do the thing absolutely backwards or upside down, and still win. There is always the golfer who, after reading the definitive way to hold a club, will reverse the position of his hands and sink the putt. There is the futures trader who makes a lot of money while totally disregarding the trend, disdaining protective stops, and overtrading. Haven't we all, at some time, wondered how this sort of anomaly could ever happen? But, the fact that some golfer can sink a putt while holding his club reversed or a futures trader make some money by ignoring the rules doesn't prove a thing. It may just be further confirmation, as if we needed additional proof, that strange or unusual things sometimes manage to occur. But, and here's the point, they don't happen very often! And you can't count on them happening, either.

My answer to the iconoclastic individual who seeks futures profits while violating most of the proven precepts of sound strategy and money management is to quote Damon Runyon. "The race may not always go to the swift, nor the contest to the strong, *but that's the way you want to bet.*" So, in your gardening, your poetry, your sculpture, or your cooking, be as uninhibited as you dare, break all the rules or invent a few of your own, and think of *discipline* as just another word in the dictionary. But, in your futures trading, play by the rules in a disciplined and pragmatic manner, trying to keep in step with the trend, which really is your friend. Keep your losses under control and don't try to pick off major tops and bottoms. And let the margin clerk or the equity run tell you when your are wrong. Be sure to heed the warning because "he who takes a small loss and runs away, lives to make big money another day." You must train yourself to ignore any personal bias towards the long side of the market because, as you have undoubtedly learned many (expensive) times, "they slide faster than they glide." You must be able to position yourself short for the slide just as easily and comfortably as you position yourself long for the glide. Whenever you have the urge to experiment, to develop new strategies or trading rules, I would be the first person to encourage that kind of individuality. By all means go for it—but test it on paper, on your computer, and in hypothetical trading. When you're in there with real money, it's not the time to experiment with theories or unproven strategies. The price of failure is too steep. Stick to what has been proven to work in the real market with real trades and real dollars.

Finally, I hope that this book will help you to look at markets in a new light. If I have done my job as author effectively, you will have more self-confidence in your ability to trade profitably. You will trade the major trends, you will control your losses while letting profits run, and you will adhere to the strictest pragmatism and discipline in your operations. If you recall and practice these and the myriad other strategies and tactics presented here, you are going to do better in your trading. You will score better profits on your winning positions and suffer smaller losses on your adverse positions. And that all adds up to better bottom-line results.

Oh, and two more things. Thanks for reading my book, and GOOD LUCK!

List of Long-Term Monthly Charts

CRB Futures Price Index

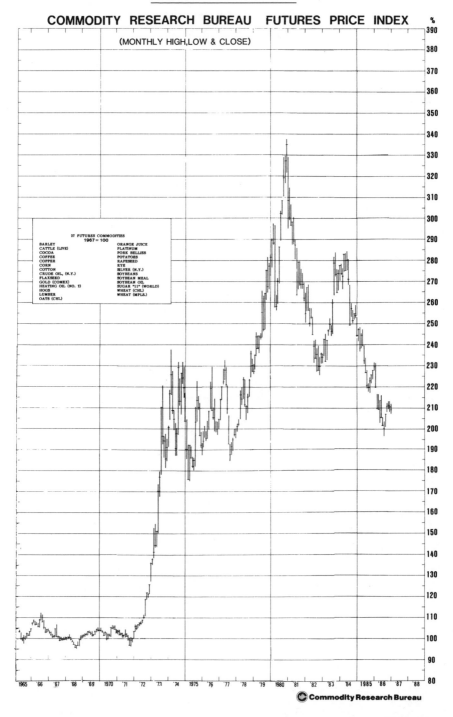

COMMODITY RESEARCH BUREAU   FUTURES   PRICE   INDEX   %

(MONTHLY HIGH,LOW & CLOSE)

27 FUTURES COMMODITIES
1967 = 100

BARLEY	ORANGE JUICE
CATTLE (LIVE)	PLATINUM
COCOA	PORK BELLIES
COFFEE	POTATOES
COPPER	RAPESEED
CORN	RYE
COTTON	SILVER (N.Y.)
CRUDE OIL, (N.Y.)	SOYBEANS
FLAXSEED	SOYBEAN MEAL
GOLD (COMEX)	SOYBEAN OIL
HEATING OIL (NO. 2)	SUGAR "11" (WORLD)
HOGS	WHEAT (CHI.)
LUMBER	WHEAT (MPLS.)
OATS (CHI.)	

© Commodity Research Bureau

Cattle (live beef)

Where traded	Chicago Mercantile Exchange, Chicago
Trading hours (New York time)	10:05 A.M. to 2:00 P.M.
Contract size	40,000 pounds
How price is quoted	Cents per pound
Minimum fluctuation:	
Per pound	2 ½/100 cent
Per contract	$10.00
Value 1 cent move:	$400
Maximum trading limit from previous close	1.50 cents (equals $600)

CATTLE (LIVE) CME CHI. (MONTHLY HIGH, LOW & CLOSE OF NEAREST FUTURES) CENTS PER POUND

Commodity Research Bureau

Cocoa

Where traded	Coffee, Sugar and Cocoa Exchange, New York
Trading hours	9:30 A.M. to 2:15 P.M.
(New York time)	
Contract size	10 tonnes
How price is quoted	Dollars per tonne
Minimum fluctuation:	
Per tonne	$1.00
Per contract	$10.00
Value $1.00 move	$10.00
Maximum trading limit	
from previous close	$88.00 (equals $880)

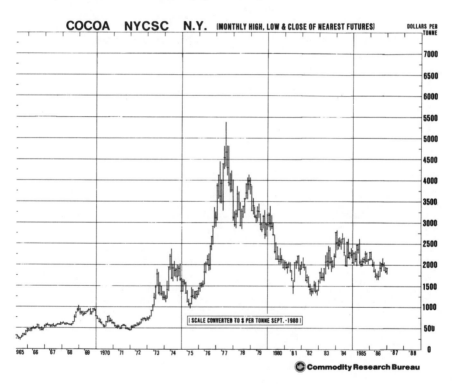

COCOA   NYCSC   N.Y.   (MONTHLY HIGH, LOW & CLOSE OF NEAREST FUTURES)   DOLLARS PER TONNE

[SCALE CONVERTED TO $ PER TONNE SEPT.-1980]

Commodity Research Bureau

Coffee

Where traded	Coffee, Sugar and Cocoa Exchange, New York
Trading hours	9:45 A.M. to 2:28 P.M.
(New York time)	
Contract size	37,500 pounds
How price is quoted	Dollars and cents per pound
Minimum fluctuation	
Per pound	1/100 cent
Per contract	$3.75
Value 1 cent move	$375.00
Maximum trading limit	
from previous close	4.00 cents (equals $1,500)
	No limit spot month

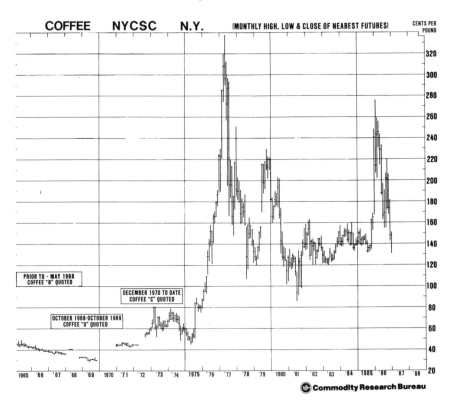

COFFEE NYCSC N.Y. (MONTHLY HIGH, LOW & CLOSE OF NEAREST FUTURES) CENTS PER POUND

PRIOR TO - MAY 1968 COFFEE "B" QUOTED

DECEMBER 1970 TO DATE COFFEE "C" QUOTED

OCTOBER 1968-OCTOBER 1969 COFFEE "U" QUOTED

1965 '66 '67 '68 '69 1970 '71 '72 '73 '74 1975 '76 '77 '78 '79 1980 '81 '82 '83 '84 1985 '86 '87 '88

Commodity Research Bureau

Copper

Where traded	Commodity Exchange, New York
Trading hours	9:25 A.M. to 2:00 P.M.
(New York time)	
Contract size	25,000 pounds
How price is quoted	Dollars and cents per pound
Minimum fluctuation	
Per pound	⁵/₁₀₀ cent
Per contract	$12.50
Value 1 cent move	$250.00
Maximum trading limit	
from previous close	5.00 cents (equals $1,250)

COPPER   COMEX   N.Y. (MONTHLY HIGH, LOW & CLOSE OF NEAREST FUTURES) CENTS PER POUND

Commodity Research Bureau

Corn

Where traded	Chicago Board of Trade, Chicago
Trading hours	10:30 A.M. to 2:15 P.M.
(New York time)	
Contract size	5,000 bushels
How price is quoted	Dollars and cents per bushel
Minimum fluctuation	
Per bushel	¼ cent
Per contract	$12.50
Value 1 cent move	$50.00
Maximum trading limit	
from previous close	10.00 cents (equals $500)

CORN   CBT   CHI.   (MONTHLY HIGH, LOW & CLOSE OF NEAREST FUTURES)   CENTS PER BUSHEL

© Commodity Research Bureau

Cotton

Where traded	New York Cotton Exchange, New York
Trading hours	10:30 A.M. to 3:00 P.M.
(New York time)	
Contract size	50,000 pounds
How price is quoted	Cents per pound
Minimum fluctuation	
Per pound	$\frac{1}{100}$ cent
Per contract	$5.00
Value 1 cent move	$500.00
Maximum trading limit	
from previous close	2.00 cents (equals $1,000)

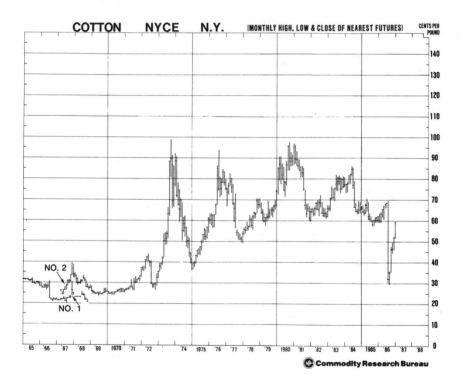

COTTON   NYCE   N.Y.   (MONTHLY HIGH, LOW & CLOSE OF NEAREST FUTURES)   CENTS PER POUND

NO. 2

NO. 1

65 '66 '67 '68 '69 1970 '71 '72 '74 1975 '76 '77 '78 '79 1980 '81 '82 '83 '84 1985 '86 '87 '88

Commodity Research Bureau

Crude Oil

Where traded	New York Mercantile Exchange, New York
Trading hours	9:45 A.M. to 3:10 P.M.
(New York time)	
Contract size	1,000 barrels (42,000 gallons)
How price is quoted	Dollars per barrel
Minimum fluctuation	
Per barrel	1 cent per barrel
Per contract	$10.00
Value $1.00 move	$1,000.00
Maximum trading limit	
from previous close	$1.00 per barrel (equals $1,000)

CRUDE OIL NYMEX N.Y. $ BARREL

Commodity Research Bureau

British Pound

Where traded	Chicago Mercantile Exchange (IMM) Chicago
Trading hours (New York time)	8:20 A.M. to 2:24 P.M.
Contract size	25,000 BP
How price is quoted	Dollars per BP
Minimum fluctuation per .05	$12.50
Value 100-point move	$250.00
Maximum trading limit from previous close	No limit

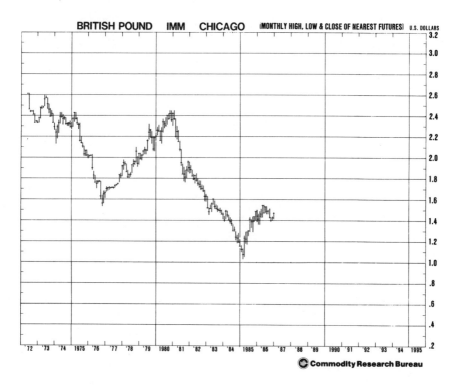

BRITISH POUND IMM CHICAGO (MONTHLY HIGH, LOW & CLOSE OF NEAREST FUTURES) U.S. DOLLARS

Commodity Research Bureau

Swiss Franc

Where traded	Chicago Mercantile Exchange (IMM) Chicago
Trading hours (New York time)	8:20 A.M. to 2:16 P.M.
Contract size	125,000 SF
How price is quoted	Dollars per SF
Minimum fluctuation per .01	$12.50
Value 100-point move	$1,250
Maximum trading limit from previous close	No limit

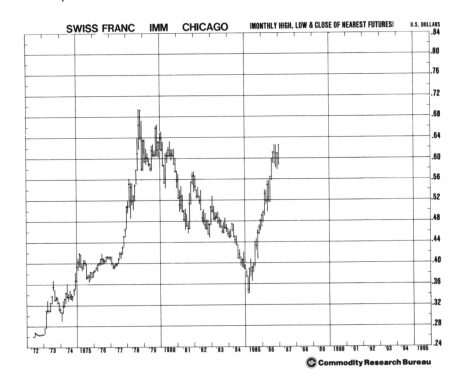

SWISS FRANC   IMM   CHICAGO   (MONTHLY HIGH, LOW & CLOSE OF NEAREST FUTURES)   U.S. DOLLARS

Commodity Research Bureau

D-Mark

Where traded	Chicago Mercantile Exchange (IMM) Chicago
Trading hours (New York time)	8:20 A.M. to 2:20 P.M.
Contract size	125,000 D-M
How price is quoted	Dollars per D-M
Minimum fluctuation per .01	$12.50
Value 100-point move	$1,250
Maximum trading limit from previous close	No limit

DEUTSCHE MARK   IMM   CHICAGO (MONTHLY HIGH, LOW & CLOSE OF NEAREST FUTURES) U.S. DOLLARS

© Commodity Research Bureau

Japanese Yen

Where traded	Chicago Mercantile Exchange (IMM) Chicago
Trading hours (New York time)	8:20 A.M. to 2:22 P.M.
Contract size	12,500,000 yen
How price is quoted	Dollars per yen
Minimum fluctuation per .0001	$12.50
Value 100-point move	$1,250.00
Maximum trading limit from previous close	No limit

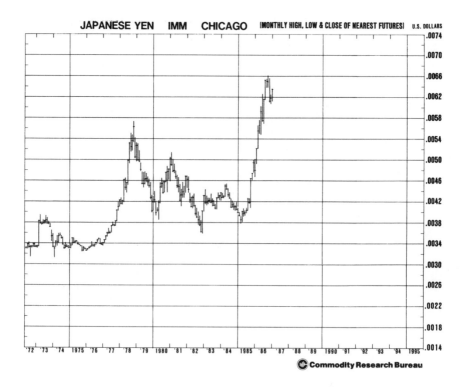

JAPANESE YEN   IMM   CHICAGO   (MONTHLY HIGH, LOW & CLOSE OF NEAREST FUTURES)   U.S. DOLLARS

Commodity Research Bureau

Gold (NY)

Where traded	Commodity Exchange, New York
Trading hours (New York time)	8:20 A.M. to 2:30 P.M.
Contract size	100 troy ounces
How price is quoted	Dollars and cents per troy ounce
Minimum fluctuation	
Per ounce	10 cents
Per contract	$10.00
Value $1.00 move	$100.00
Maximum trading limit from previous close	$25.00 per troy ounce (equals $2,500)

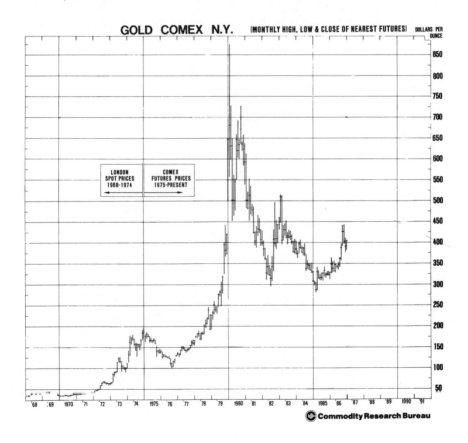

GOLD COMEX N.Y. (MONTHLY HIGH, LOW & CLOSE OF NEAREST FUTURES) DOLLARS PER OUNCE

LONDON SPOT PRICES 1968-1974

COMEX FUTURES PRICES 1975-PRESENT

© Commodity Research Bureau

Heating Oil

Where traded	New York Mercantile Exchange, New York
Trading hours	9:50 A.M. to 3:05 P.M.
(New York time)	
Contract size	1,000 barrels (42,000 gallons)
How price is quoted	Dollars per gallon
Minimum fluctuation	
Per gallon	$\frac{1}{100}$ cent
Per contract	$4.20
Value 1 cent move	$420.00
Maximum trading limit	
from previous close	2 cents per gallon (equals $840)

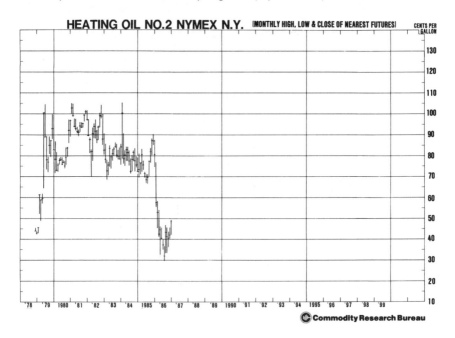

HEATING OIL NO.2 NYMEX N.Y. (MONTHLY HIGH, LOW & CLOSE OF NEAREST FUTURES)   CENTS PER GALLON

© Commodity Research Bureau

Hogs (live)

Where traded	Chicago Mercantile Exchange, Chicago
Trading hours	10:10 A.M. to 2:00 P.M.
(New York time)	
Contract size	30,000 pounds
How price is quoted	Cents per pound
Minimum fluctuation	
Per pound	2 ½/100 cent
Per contract	$7.50
Value 1 cent move	$300.00
Maximum trading limit	
from previous close	1.50 cents (equals $450)

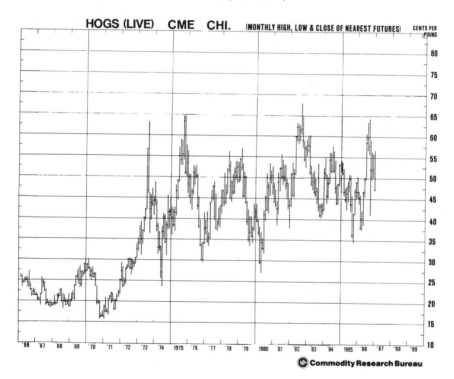

HOGS (LIVE)   CME   CHI.   (MONTHLY HIGH, LOW & CLOSE OF NEAREST FUTURES)   CENTS PER POUND

Commodity Research Bureau

Lumber

Where traded	Chicago Mercantile Exchange, Chicago
Trading hours (New York time)	10:00 A.M. to 2:05 P.M.
Contract size	130,000 board feet
How price is quoted	Dollars per 1,000 board feet
Minimum fluctuation	
Per 1,000 board feet	10 cents
Per contract	$13.00
Value $1.00 move	$130.00
Maximum trading limit from previous close	$5.00 per 1,000 board feet (equals $650)

LUMBER   CME   CHI.   (MONTHLY HIGH, LOW & CLOSE OF NEAREST FUTURES)   DOLLARS PER 1,000 SQ. FT.

© Commodity Research Bureau

Platinum

Where traded	New York Mercantile Exchange, New York
Trading hours	8:20 A.M. to 2:30 P.M.
(New York time)	
Contract size	50 troy ounces
How price is quoted	Dollars and cents per troy ounce
Minimum fluctuation	
Per ounce	10.00 cents
Per contract	$5.00
Value $1.00 move	$50.00
Maximum trading limit	
from previous close	$25.00 (equals $1,250)

PLATINUM   NYMEX   N.Y.   (MONTHLY HIGH, LOW & CLOSE OF NEAREST FUTURES)   DOLLARS PER OUNCE

HIGH–1045

© Commodity Research Bureau

Pork Bellies

Where traded	Chicago Mercantile Exchange, Chicago
Trading hours	10:10 A.M. to 2:00 P.M.
(New York time)	
Contract size	40,000 pounds
How price is quoted	Cents per pound
Minimum fluctuation	
Per pound	2 ½/100 cent
Per contract	$10.00
Value 1 cent move	$400.00
Maximum trading limit	
from previous close	2.00 cents (equals $800)

PORK BELLIES   CME   CHI.   (MONTHLY HIGH, LOW & CLOSE OF NEAREST FUTURES)   CENTS PER POUND

Commodity Research Bureau

S&P 500 Index

Where traded	Chicago Mercantile Exchange (IMM) Chicago
Trading hours (New York time)	9:30 A.M. to 4:15 P.M.
Contract size	$500 × index
How price is quoted	Index
Minimum fluctuation per .05	$25.00
Value 100-point move	$500.00
Maximum trading limit from previous close	No limit

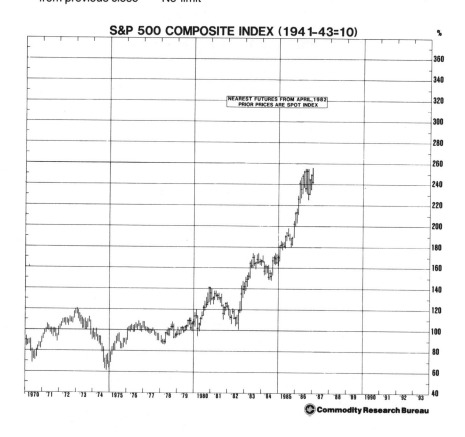

S&P 500 COMPOSITE INDEX (1941-43=10)

NEAREST FUTURES FROM APRIL, 1982
PRIOR PRICES ARE SPOT INDEX

Commodity Research Bureau

Silver (NY)

Where traded	Commodity Exchange, New York
Trading hours	8:25 A.M. to 2:25 P.M.
(New York time)	
Contract size	5,000 troy ounces
How price is quoted	Dollars and cents per troy ounce
Minimum fluctuation	
Per ounce	$^{10}\!/_{100}$ cent
Per contract	$5.00
Value 1 cent move	$50.00
Maximum trading limit	
from previous close	50.00 cents (equals $2,500)

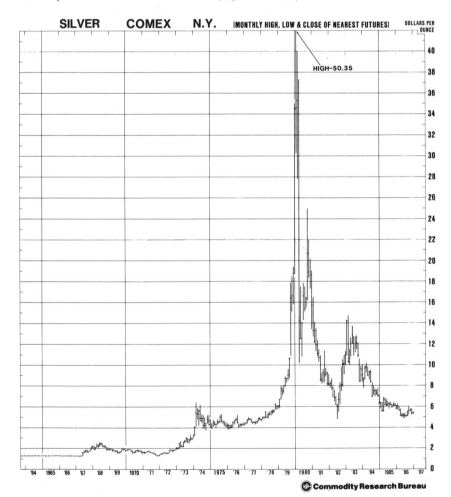

SILVER   COMEX   N.Y.   (MONTHLY HIGH, LOW & CLOSE OF NEAREST FUTURES)   DOLLARS PER OUNCE

HIGH–50.35

Soybeans

Where traded	Chicago Board of Trade, Chicago
Trading hours (New York time)	10:30 A.M. to 2:15 P.M.
Contract size	5,000 bushels
How price is quoted	Dollars and cents per bushel
Minimum fluctuation	
Per bushel	¼ cent
Per contract	$12.50
Value 1 cent move	$50.00
Maximum trading limit from previous close	30 cents (equals $1,500)

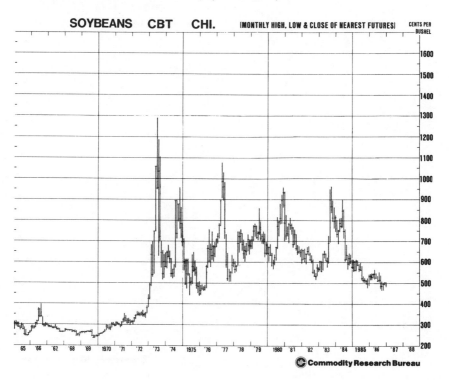

SOYBEANS CBT CHI. (MONTHLY HIGH, LOW & CLOSE OF NEAREST FUTURES) CENTS PER BUSHEL

Commodity Research Bureau

Soybean Meal

Where traded	Chicago Board of Trade, Chicago
Trading hours	10:30 A.M. to 2:15 P.M.
(New York time)	
Contract size	100 tons
How price is quoted	Dollars and cents per ton
Minimum fluctuation	
Per ton	10 cents
Per contract	$10.00
Value $1.00 move	$100.00
Maximum trading limit	
from previous close	$10.00 (equals $1,000)

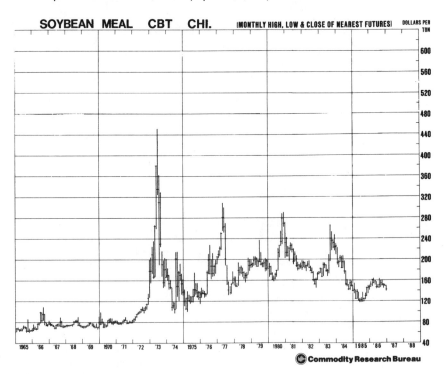

SOYBEAN MEAL CBT CHI. (MONTHLY HIGH, LOW & CLOSE OF NEAREST FUTURES) DOLLARS PER TON

Commodity Research Bureau

Soybean Oil

Where traded	Chicago Board of Trade, Chicago
Trading hours	10:30 A.M. to 2:15 P.M.
(New York time)	
Contract size	60,000 pounds
How price is quoted	Cents per pound
Minimum fluctuation	
Per pound	1/100 cent
Per contract	$6.00
Value 1 cent move	$600.00
Maximum trading limit	
from previous close	1 cent (equals $600)

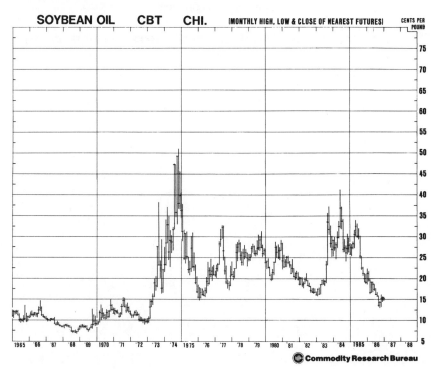

SOYBEAN OIL   CBT   CHI.   (MONTHLY HIGH, LOW & CLOSE OF NEAREST FUTURES)   CENTS PER POUND

© Commodity Research Bureau

Sugar (world)

Where traded	Coffee, Sugar and Cocoa Exchange, New York
Trading hours (New York time)	10:00 A.M. to 1:43 P.M.
Contract size	112,000 pounds
How price is quoted	Cents per pound
Minimum fluctuation	
Per pound	$1/100$ cent
Per contract	$11.20
Value 1 cent move	$1,120.00
Maximum trading limit from previous close	1/2 cent (equals $560) No limit first two contracts

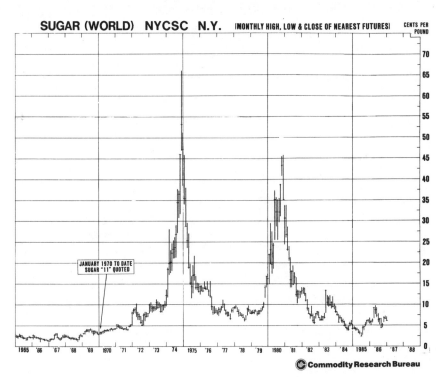

SUGAR (WORLD) NYCSC N.Y. [MONTHLY HIGH, LOW & CLOSE OF NEAREST FUTURES] CENTS PER POUND

JANUARY 1970 TO DATE SUGAR "11" QUOTED

⚫ **Commodity Research Bureau**

Wheat (Chicago)

Where traded	Chicago Board of Trade, Chicago
Trading hours (New York time)	10:30 A.M. to 2:15 P.M.
Contract size	5,000 bushels
How price is quoted	Dollars and cents per bushel
Minimum fluctuation	
Per bushel	¼ cent
Per contract	$12.50
Value 1 cent move	$50.00
Maximum trading limit from previous close	20 cents (equals $1,000)

WHEAT   CBT   CHICAGO   (MONTHLY HIGH, LOW & CLOSE OF NEAREST FUTURES)   CENTS PER BUSHEL

Ⓒ **Commodity Research Bureau**

T-Bills

Where traded	Chicago Mercantile Exchange (IMM) Chicago
Trading hours (New York time)	8:20 A.M. to 3:00 P.M.
Contract size	$1,000,000
How price is quoted	Points of 100%
Minimum fluctuation per .01	$25.00
Value 100-point move	$2,500
Maximum trading limit from previous close	No limit

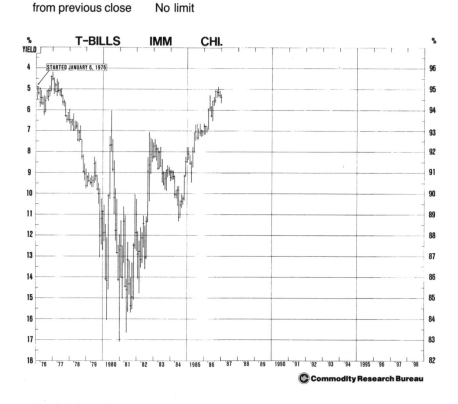

Commodity Research Bureau

T-Bonds

Where traded	Chicago Board of Trade, Chicago
Trading hours	9:00 A.M. to 3:00 P.M.
(New York time)	
Contract size	$100,000
How price is quoted	Points 32nds of 100%
Minimum fluctuation	
per 1/32 point	$31.25
Value 100-point move (32/32)	$1,000
Maximum trading limit	
from previous close	96/32 (equals $3,000)

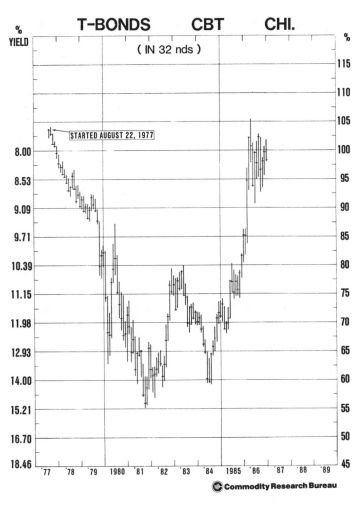

Commodity Research Bureau

Value Line Index

Where traded	Kansas City Board of Trade, Kansas City
Trading hours (New York time)	9:30 A.M. to 4:15 P.M.
Contract size	$500 × index
How price is quoted	Index
Minimum fluctuation per .05	$25.00
Value 100-point move	$500.00
Maximum trading limit from previous close	No limit

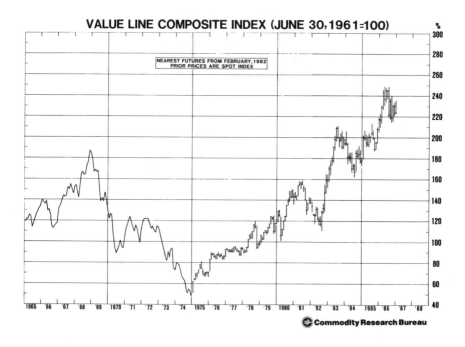

VALUE LINE COMPOSITE INDEX (JUNE 30, 1961=100)

NEAREST FUTURES FROM FEBRUARY, 1982
PRIOR PRICES ARE SPOT INDEX

Commodity Research Bureau

Index